To:

....

From:

....

Date:

....

THE
100-DAY
PRAYER
GUIDE
FOR TEEN GUYS

ELIJAH ADKINS

THE
100-DAY
PRAYER
GUIDE
FOR TEEN GUYS

BARBOUR
PUBLISHING

Published by Barbour Publishing, Inc., 1810 Barbour Drive, Uhrichsville, Ohio 44683, www.barbourbooks.com

Our mission is to inspire the world with the life-changing message of the Bible.

Member of the
Evangelical Christian
Publishers Association

Printed in China.

GET ON THE ROAD TO A MORE POWERFUL PRAYER LIFE

The 100-Day Prayer Guide for Teen Guys offers relatable, real-life wisdom and inspiration for prayer. You'll encounter page after page of biblical truths you can apply to your own quiet time with God.

It covers overarching topics like Praise, Confession, and Intercession, as well as more specific issues, such as

- family
- culture
- the lost
- healing
- physical needs
- and much more.

This book provides a biblical example or teaching on each subject, a helpful devotional thought, guidance on incorporating the topic into your own prayer life, and a brief prayer starter.

It's a perfect way to spend your next hundred days!

1.
A GOOD PLACE

*I cried to the Lord in my trouble, and He
answered me and put me in a good place.*
PSALM 118:5 NLV

We all know the world that God made is beautiful, filled with exotic expressions of His infinite creativity. But just as every rose has its thorn, so this world can often seem. . .not so beautiful. Relationships dissolve. Family members grow ill. Hearts are crushed. Bones are broken. Sometimes it seems a stretch to refer to this world as a good place at all.

But that's where God comes in. He knows this life can be hard—intolerable at times. He knows how pain often overshadows the beauty. He knows because He's been here. He walked among us in this bittersweet place. Why? So He could lead us to someplace better.

When we pray, we form a bridge between our pain and God's goodness—a direct line of communication with the only one who can solve our problems. Physically, we'll remain on this earth until the end of our lives. But our spirits are transported into God's infinite goodness every time we open our hearts to Him in prayer.

THINK ABOUT IT

- How can times of stress and uncertainty strengthen your prayer life?

- What pains or sorrows are you facing—or are you worried about facing—today?

- When was the last time you sought out God's "good place" in prayer?

PRAY ABOUT IT

- Pray today, even when your problems seem trivial.

- Pray that God will keep you in His "good place."

- Pray as often as you can—in class, at home, with your friends, whenever.

Lord Jesus, thank You for leading me into Your goodness whenever my current situation is anything but good.

2.
EVERYONE'S WATCHING

*About midnight Paul and Silas were praying
and singing songs of thanks to God. The other
men in prison were listening to them.*
ACTS 16:25 NLV

At its core, prayer is a private means of communication with God. But just because prayer is solely between you and God, does that mean nobody will ever notice? Of course not!

If you regularly pray over your food before lunch, other teens in the cafeteria will eventually notice. If you are truly thankful to God for His blessings, gratitude will pour out in your speech. In short, consistent prayer and thanksgiving to God are impossible to hide, even if you're not doing anything to be seen.

Just like the other prisoners took notice of Paul and Silas' inexplicable gratitude, so your friends and everyone you see each day will eventually notice how you respond to various situations. If you say you're a Christian and yet complain every time a minor inconvenience arises, they'll spot the hypocrisy. But if you profess your faith and then respond to everything—even tragedies—with prayer and gratitude, others will take note of your faith in action.

And perhaps, just maybe, they'll start wanting what you have.

THINK ABOUT IT

- Are you embarrassed to pray in public? Why or why not?

- What do you think when you see someone else praying?

- Why is it important to pray as if nobody's watching, even if someone is?

PRAY ABOUT IT

- Thank God in every situation, no matter who's present.

- Ask God for increased courage to show your faith in public.

- Pray that God will use you to be a positive example to someone who needs it.

God, give me the unabashed optimism of Paul and Silas, even when gratitude might seem like a strange response.

3.
ARTIFICIAL PRAYERS

*"But when you pray, do not use vain repetitions
as the heathen do. For they think that they
shall be heard for their many words."*
MATTHEW 6:7 SKJV

If yesterday's verse proved how important it is to never hide your faith, today's verse tells us to avoid the other end of the spectrum: flaunting your prayer life to be noticed.

Paul and Silas' prayers were noticed because their words flowed from their hearts, and they made no effort to hide them. Prayer was as natural as breathing for them. The "heathen" mentioned in today's verse, however, wear their faith like a mask, seeking to score points with the people they think will appreciate it. And then when they encounter people who might look down on their faith, they strip off the mask and reveal their true face—worldliness and spiritual apathy.

Prayer isn't a magic show or circus performance. If it doesn't flow from the heart, it's best that it doesn't flow at all. When you're truly looking to God, you'll never have the urge to shout, "Look at me!"

THINK ABOUT IT

- When was the last time you prayed in public? What was your motivation?

- Why is vain prayer often more harmful than no prayer at all?

- How easy is it for you to tell when someone's prayer is sincere or merely a show?

PRAY ABOUT IT

- Ask God to give you a right attitude toward prayer.

- Pray for God to reveal any wrong motivation for prayer that may lie in your heart.

- When you pray, focus solely on God rather than on who might be watching.

Lord, I never want to make a mockery of Your greatest gift to humanity: the ability to have a personal connection with You. May my prayers be genuine, not artificial.

4.
PRAYER AND POLITICS

Pray for kings and all others who are in power over
us so we might live quiet God-like lives in peace.
1 TIMOTHY 2:2 NLV

What do you think about politics? Do you find it fascinating or hardly give it a thought? Whatever your viewpoint, if you're not yet old enough to vote, you really don't have any say in the process.

Except. . .that isn't quite true. Today's verse was written during a time when there were no presidents or checks and balances. Rome had an emperor appointed not by elections but by bloodline or conquest. But despite all this, Paul knew there *was* a way Christians could make a difference in government—through prayer.

Prayer wasn't just a formality—a routine uttering of "God save the king." No, it was a way for these early Christians to ensure that the decisions that happened in royal palaces would be divinely approved.

Today, if there's one thing our leaders need more than votes, it's prayer. Are you willing to go to God on their behalf?

THINK ABOUT IT

- Do you forget that politicians and leaders are people too? Why or why not?

- Does God ever use bad leaders to bring about good results?

- If you were in a position of authority, wouldn't you want others to pray for you?

PRAY ABOUT IT

- Ask God to guide the leaders of your country in the direction He wants them to go.

- Pray that the unsaved men and women in leadership roles will come to know Christ.

- Pray that these leaders will be concerned for what's right, not for selfish gain.

Father, guide the people who guide this country.
Fill their hearts with a love for Your righteousness,
and show them the path they should take.

5.
PERSECUTION

*So Peter was held in prison. But the
church kept praying to God for him.*
ACTS 12:5 NLV

Religious persecution is a lot less prevalent in modern western society. At worst, Christians may receive a dirty glance or harsh word from time to time. Compared to the way things were long ago, little physical danger exists.

But in many countries, even today, Christianity is illegal—and the punishment for disobedience is far harsher than the one described in today's verse. Believers are tortured, beheaded, and ripped away from their families—all for believing in Jesus as their Savior.

Clearly, when it comes to persecuted Christians, there's still a lot to pray about. It helps to read books, watch movies, or find news articles that deal with the topic of persecution. Why? To prevent us from becoming apathetic. By placing ourselves in their shoes, we can pray more fervently for their protection and—most importantly—their endurance in the face of suffering and even death. And maybe to be prepared for increasingly bad conditions in our own nation.

THINK ABOUT IT

- How do you respond when you hear about Christians being persecuted?

- How can you make sure you never view persecution as a distant problem?

- Does your prayer list include those who are facing persecution?

PRAY ABOUT IT

- Ask God to give you a heart for suffering believers.

- Pray for God to either rescue them or give them peace.

- Try to remember specific names and pray for them regularly.

Father, please protect Christians who are suffering for their faith. Give them the courage and peace to stick with You, our eternal hope.

6.
SPONTANEOUS PRAYER

*Evening and morning and at noon I will pray
and cry aloud, and He shall hear my voice.*
PSALM 55:17 SKJV

It's easy to treat prayer like just another ritual we do before bedtime—a string of words that finish out the day and prepare us for sleep. But while it is important to establish a time of daily prayer, your time with God should by no means be limited to set schedules.

No matter where you are, what you're doing, or how big your problem is, God is always waiting to hear your voice. Running behind and fearing you'll be late for class? Pray. Worried that tomorrow's test might tank your grade? Pray. Sick of getting bullied by that guy in math class? You guessed it, pray. Even when the problems grow into mountains or potential tragedies, prayer will always be the right response.

Often, the specific answer to these prayers is less important than the fact that you prayed. By making prayer more of an immediate reaction than a repetitive routine, you'll be on your way to deepening your relationship with God.

THINK ABOUT IT

- Do you talk to your friends only about the same things at the same time each day?

- Does your prayer life fit into a mold, or is it spontaneous and personal?

- How might conversations with friends serve as models for prayer?

PRAY ABOUT IT

- Look for reasons to pray today.

- Ask God to deepen your understanding of what prayer actually is.

- Pray about concerns you would never mention to anyone else.

---

*Father, I want my relationship with
You to be spontaneous and genuine.
Give me a passion for prayer.*

7.
THE SOLUTION FOR STRESS

Be anxious for nothing, but in everything,
by prayer and supplication with thanksgiving,
let your requests be made known to God.
PHILIPPIANS 4:6 SKJV

All anxiety has its source in uncertainty. Often, that uncertainty is sparked by something new or unexpected—a difficult class, a new relationship, a conflict with a friend. And when left to fester in the back of your mind, these thoughts can grow absurdly dramatic, disconnected from any sense of reality.

That's why this verse tells us to bring our requests to God. Psychologists agree that the mere act of giving voice to your anxiety can put things into perspective and calm the storm inside—and who better to share your worries with than the Creator of all things?

Even more, modern neuroscience (the scientific study of the nervous system) has also discovered that showing gratitude, even when it seems like there's nothing to be thankful for at the moment, can dramatically decrease stress levels. And once again, who could possibly deserve our gratitude more than the one who gave us everything?

Worry may be a powerful force, but prayer is the solution to stress.

THINK ABOUT IT

- Do you try to escape worry, or do you wallow in it each time it comes?
- How can you remind yourself to pray and give thanks when stressed?
- What were some "hopeless" situations in which you came through just fine?

PRAY ABOUT IT

- Ask God to help you see His power instead of your weakness.
- Make a list of all the things you're glad God has given you, then thank Him.
- Thank God in advance for bringing you through yet another struggle.

Without You, God, I'd be a mess for sure.
Thank You for giving me an anchor when
everything else feels so unsteady.

8.
FOOLISH BEHAVIOR

I want men everywhere to pray. They should lift up holy hands as they pray. They should not be angry or argue.
1 TIMOTHY 2:8 NLV

To better understand how prayer is the remedy to conflict, imagine that a couple of citizens have been summoned before the throne room of their king. Out of the kindness of his heart, the ruler has given both men an enormous sum of money. But instead of being thankful, the two citizens immediately begin fighting with each other over who got more money—right in front of the king.

As foolish as this scenario seems, isn't that what many of us Christians do? God has given us so many blessings, and yet we want to quibble and quarrel over the smallest of details. This humiliates us and disrespects God in the process.

The only solution for such self-destructive behavior is to turn our arguments into prayers. By going to God with thanksgiving, we can drown out the contentious voices that threaten to ruin our relationship with Him and the people He's placed in our lives.

THINK ABOUT IT

- How do you respond when you feel upset with someone?

- When was the last time you lashed out in anger? Did it solve anything?

- Imagine yourself as a citizen at God's throne. Is He pleased by your behavior?

PRAY ABOUT IT

- When you feel jealous of someone, thank God for what you *do* have.

- When you feel angry over a perceived wrong, ask God for the strength to forgive.

- When you have a disagreement, thank God for putting up with your own errors.

Lord, all my grievances are nothing compared to the thanksgiving I owe You. Show me how to turn toward You and away from potential conflicts.

9.
DON'T BULLY THE BULLY

*"Pray for those who do bad things to you
and who make it hard for you."*
MATTHEW 5:44 NLV

Nobody likes a bully. They stand in the hallways and prey on the weak and innocent, usually in order to hide the insecurity they feel themselves. And if you think that bullies will disappear once you finish high school, think again. Bullies can be found everywhere you look—from greedy coworkers to political leaders to mere trolls on the internet. If you're breathing, you're probably being bullied in some way or another.

Jesus understood this truth, but He also knew that prayer is the best defense against letting ourselves take this bullying to heart. You see, our real battle is often not against the bullies but with our response to them. The moment you respond in kind is the moment you give up any hope of breaking the cycle.

When you pray for those who hurt you, three things are accomplished: (1) you feel better about yourself, (2) you please God, and (3) you shine a light on the very one who's causing the pain.

Today, don't bully the bully—pray for him instead.

THINK ABOUT IT

- Why is the notion of praying for bullies countercultural?

- How does fighting back often make things worse?

- How might learning about the bully's life enable you to pray sincerely for him?

PRAY ABOUT IT

- Ask God to help you better understand the bully's personal struggles.

- Pray that God will fill the bully's heart with love instead of bitterness.

- Pray for the strength to respond gracefully each time.

Lord Jesus, You faced the worst humanity had to offer, and You still didn't give in to anger. Help me to have that level of love and grace.

10.
HIDDEN SINS

I said, "I will confess my transgressions to the
LORD," and You forgave the iniquity of my sin.
PSALM 32:5 SKJV

Sometimes it's easy to say, "I'm sorry." When the mistake is obvious and everyone knows about it, apologies come naturally. But in these cases, confession is often little more than damage control—a last-ditch effort to avoid making everyone angrier than they already are.

Other times, however, our sins are much more hidden—committed in solitude and kept secret from everyone. We feel guilty over them, sure, but confessing them to God seems impossible. Maybe if we don't ever bring them up, it'll be like they never happened. But such thinking only paves the way for the mistake to be repeated.

By clearly acknowledging the line you crossed, the air is suddenly cleared between you and God. You know where you stand, so you can better feel the relief that comes with His forgiveness.

Don't dread the act of confession—find peace and happiness in the freedom it provides.

THINK ABOUT IT

- What role does pride play in keeping us from confessing?

- Have you confessed *all* your sins to God, or are you holding some back?

- Why is it important to confess immediately, rather than waiting until the guilt is too much to bear?

PRAY ABOUT IT

- Pray for the humility to take your faults before God.

- Ask God to reveal sins you were not even aware of.

- Practice confessing the moment you realize your mistake.

God, I wish I could say I never sin, but that would be a lie. Please show me when I step out of line, and help me find relief in Your grace.

11.
AVENGERS. . .DISASSEMBLE

Do not avenge yourselves, dearly beloved,
but rather give place to wrath, for it is written,
"Vengeance is Mine. I will repay," says the Lord.
ROMANS 12:19 SKJV

Modern culture is fascinated by the idea of avenging wrongs. (Why else do you think the most popular superhero team is called "the Avengers"?) There's something satisfying about watching fictional evil get the punishment it deserves.

But what about in real life? Should we all aspire to be vigilantes, swiftly avenging those who wrong us? Today's verse offers a resounding no. In fact, Proverbs 24:17 says we shouldn't even rejoice when the wicked fall—whether it was our hand that caused it or not. So what should we do when the sting of injustice is burning in our hearts?

Pray.

We should pray to God—not with a spiteful, "strike 'em down" attitude, but rather an "I'm leaving this matter in Your hands" surrender. By giving up our desire for retaliation and letting God take the reins of vengeance, we can be sure that in the end, true justice will be served—if not in this life, then the next.

THINK ABOUT IT

- What's your attitude when you see bad things happen to bad people?

- What would the world be like if everyone got what they truly deserved? Would anyone have any hope?

- Why is God alone qualified to dish out vengeance?

PRAY ABOUT IT

- Practice giving your anger to God, even when it's barely noticeable.

- Pray for the wisdom to see past the quick thrill of revenge.

- Ask God to fill your heart with the same love and compassion He has for sinners.

Father, thank You for being perfectly just.
Teach me to trust Your judgment,
even when I want so badly to enact my own.

12.
ACCORDING TO PLAN

*Heal me, O Lord, and I will be healed. Save me
and I will be saved. For You are my praise.*
JEREMIAH 17:14 NLV

One misconception among Christians is that God will always heal sickness if we pray. Another misconception is that we can do nothing about sickness except let nature run its course.

Both views are false. God wants us to pray for healing—as seen in this verse and many others throughout the Bible. But we must always do so with the recognition that sometimes sickness (and even death) may be part of God's plan.

In other words, prayers for healing must have two elements: (1) humility about our own lack of understanding, and (2) confidence in God's plan and in His power to bring it about. If it's God's will to heal you or a family member, then healing will come. If not, then rest assured—He's got a better kind of healing in store for all who love Him. These temporary moments of pain and sadness are serving as mere stepping stones to this glorious future.

THINK ABOUT IT

- Have you ever felt frustrated by God's silence in response to a prayer?

- How might a better understanding of God's infinite knowledge help you grapple with these feelings?

- How is salvation the best healing of all?

PRAY ABOUT IT

- Ask God to increase your faith in His wisdom and power, always making sure to add "if it's Your will" to the end of your prayers for healing.

- Remember to thank Him each time He does provide the healing you seek.

- Thank Him even when He doesn't provide the healing you seek.

Lord, sickness is a sad reality of this world. I'm asking for Your intervention today, knowing You can do it if it's Your will. Please help me to accept whatever answer You give.

13.
DISJOINTED PRAYER

We do not know how to pray or what we should pray for, but the Holy Spirit prays to God for us with sounds that cannot be put into words.
ROMANS 8:26 NLV

The mind is a complex creation—so complex, in fact, that it's often impossible to understand its inner workings, even within ourselves.

As a teen, you probably know how terrifying your own emotions can feel—how pain, joy, and sadness can whirl like a tornado in your thoughts. Handling one emotion is hard enough—how in the world are you supposed to deal with feelings you can't even describe?

One great thing about God is that He knows you better than you know yourself. So you can always come to Him in prayer, even if your prayer consists of little more than groaning. Why? Because to Him, these confused noises are the language of a broken heart—a language He deeply comprehends. Not only will He listen to your pleas, but He'll be there to comfort you during your struggles.

Don't be afraid to take your mess to God. He's the only one who can make sense of your confusion.

THINK ABOUT IT

- Does all prayer have to be verbal? Why or why not?

- Do you often wait to sort out your own emotions before praying?

- Why might God sometimes value unorganized prayers over clearly spoken ones?

PRAY ABOUT IT

- Practice spilling your strong emotions out to God, even the ones you don't understand.

- Ask God to bring clarity to your mind's chaos.

- Thank God for hearing you when nobody else understands.

Lord, I may not understand what I'm feeling, but I know You're able to make sense of it. Thank You for listening to my disjointed pleas.

14.
WHEN WILLPOWER ISN'T ENOUGH

"Watch and pray so that you will not be tempted. Man's spirit is willing, but the body does not have the power to do it."
MATTHEW 26:41 NLV

Ever try your best to conquer some sin that's invaded your life, only to find yourself defeated each time? Ever feel like you're not powerful enough to stop your own self-destructive behaviors?

Well, that's because you aren't. But don't fret. You serve a God who is powerful enough. There's a reason the process of salvation involves the Holy Spirit coming to dwell inside us—without His presence, we'd have no hope of bettering ourselves. Sin would still be our master, and our lives would be marked by failure after failure.

But thankfully, God's power is only a prayer away. So pray today for an escape from temptation and, if temptation is unavoidable, for the strength to face it head-on. When you're all out of ammunition in your war with the devil, God's got plenty of support just waiting—all you need to do is ask.

THINK ABOUT IT

- Do you try to face temptation alone, or are you ready to admit your weakness?

- Why do you think God doesn't give us all the strength we need before we pray?

- What actions might we take to ensure we avoid tempting scenarios?

PRAY ABOUT IT

- Pray for the wisdom to remove yourself from potential temptations.

- Ask God for a proper perspective so you can choose His will when you're tempted to choose your own.

- Practice putting God first in all areas of your life so that prayer will come naturally in times of temptation.

Father, thank You for Your Spirit who
enables me to resist the irresistible.
Help me to continue choosing Your holiness.

15.
POWER IN PRAYER

"Whoever calls on the name of the Lord will be saved from the punishment of sin."
Acts 2:21 nlv

Never underestimate the value of prayer.

While many people, even some Christians, tend to treat prayer as a last resort, you must remember that prayer was the spark that lit the fire of your salvation. It was through prayer that you asked Jesus to enter your life, and it was through prayer that you sought forgiveness for your sin. And what difference did that make? The difference between life and death—eternally!

So yes, prayer *does* matter. It matters so much that God ordained it as our primary mode of communication with Him. Today, rejoice in the ability God has given you to pray. Take advantage of it every chance you get, calling on the name of the Lord for every problem you face. Forgiveness, healing, blessings, comfort, peace, love, joy, and so much more can be found through the act of praying.

What a gift!

THINK ABOUT IT

- How often do you pray?

- Why do you think we're often tempted to avoid prayer, even though it's simply talking to God?

- If God knows what we're thinking, why do you think He wants us to pray?

PRAY ABOUT IT

- Ask God for a renewed appreciation for prayer.

- Don't limit your prayers to memorized lines— tell Him what's truly on Your mind.

- Thank God for listening to each request you make.

Lord, may my requests to You flow as freely as the thoughts that cross my mind. I never want to miss the chance to speak with You.

16.
EXEMPLARY MERCY

The Lord returned to Job all the things that he had lost, when he prayed for his friends.
JOB 42:10 NLV

Earlier we talked about Jesus' command to pray for our enemies. And in today's verse, we see a perfect example of that kind of prayer in action.

Throughout the book of Job, the title character's friends compounded his misery by accusing him of sins he did not commit. So what did Job do after finally hearing the Lord's voice? Scoff and say, "I told you so"? Ask God to punish his tormentors?

No, he prayed for his persecutors. The previous verses indicate that this prayer was one of intercession—that God would *refrain* from punishing Job's three friends. Even though Job's friends had made him miserable, he did not wish this level of misery on them. He prayed and made sacrifices for them just as he would have done for himself.

Don't use your prayers as an excuse to point blame. Instead, embrace kindness in your prayers.

THINK ABOUT IT

- Have you ever been falsely accused of something? If so, what was your prayer at that time? What about after the truth came out?

- Why did God wait to return Job's blessings until after he prayed for his friends?

- How does Job's prayer remind us of Jesus' prayer on the cross?

PRAY ABOUT IT

- If someone unintentionally wrongs you, ask God to help you forgive and forget.

- If someone intentionally wrongs you, pray that this person repents.

- If someone *keeps* hurting you intentionally, pray for the grace to confront the problem in a kind, merciful way.

Lord, thank You for forgiving me of my many sins. Please help me to see others through the same eyes with which You see me.

17.
PRAYING WITH URGENCY

The end of the world is near. You must be the boss
over your mind. Keep awake so you can pray.
1 PETER 4:7 NLV

What would you do if you knew the world would end tomorrow?

Many have asked this question, and the answers are almost as varied as the number of people on the planet. Today's verse, however, says that the most important thing we can do is pray—pray for forgiveness for unrepented sins, for the salvation of those who are lost, for the wisdom to live these final moments in the way God wants us to. Since we don't know when the end of the world will come, it could well *be* tomorrow. . .or tonight. . .or five seconds from now.

See the urgency?

Pray like each minute might be your last. Stay in good standing with God, keeping up your end of the conversation. That way, when Jesus finally comes in the clouds, it'll be like reuniting with a close friend you've been looking forward to seeing.

THINK ABOUT IT

- If Jesus came back right now, can you think of anything you wish you would have prayed about?

- If so, what's stopping you from praying about it right now?

- How can you get rid of the "I've got all the time in the world to pray" mindset?

PRAY ABOUT IT

- Ask God to make Jesus' Second Coming relevant in your mind.

- Pray that God will use you to accomplish His plan before the end comes.

- Pray that as many people as possible will come to know Him before time runs out.

Lord, I don't know when the end will come, but I'm going to live—and pray—like it's tomorrow. Teach me to pray with urgency.

18.
FAULTY REPENTANCE

The people of Israel cried out to the Lord, saying,
"We have sinned against You. We have turned
away from our God and are serving the Baals."
JUDGES 10:10 NLV

Reading today's verse out of context, it can be tempting to assume it comes right after the punishment. After all, isn't that the way it usually works? You do something wrong, get caught, receive punishment, and immediately apologize. Then everything returns to normal, and you walk away having learned a valuable lesson.

Unfortunately, none of this applied to Israel. Verse 8 reveals they'd been oppressed for *eighteen years* before they finally came to their senses. . .and then they fell right back into sin.

So what can we learn from Israel's prayer? Well, our confessions should follow this prayer's form—we should bare our hearts before God, admitting where we went wrong and seeking His forgiveness. But as for everything else, it's a case study in what *not* to do. Don't wait years before confessing, and don't confess solely out of a desire to escape your punishment so you can jump right back into your sin.

Let your confessions be quick and genuine as you trust in God's power to forgive.

THINK ABOUT IT

- How can we gain a sincere attitude of repentance?

- Is it ever too late to repent? Too early?

- How might Israel's story have been different if they repented immediately?

PRAY ABOUT IT

- Ask God to help you recognize flaws in your heart before they grow.

- Pray for the humility to repent sincerely.

- Ask for God to remind you of your past repentance when you're tempted to make the same mistakes.

God, thank You for second chances.
May I use Your grace as an opportunity to
rebound into a closer walk with You.

19.
HONOR AND RESPECT

Honor your father and your mother, that your days may be long on the land that the LORD your God gives you.
EXODUS 20:12 SKJV

There are many ways to fulfill today's command. Obedience, of course, is the most obvious one. . .but what about prayer?

If you think about it, bringing someone's name before the King of the universe—both in thanksgiving and to ask for that person's well-being—is probably the most profound way you can honor that person. This is especially true for parents (or grandparents, or guardians, or whoever might be raising you). They've chosen to sacrifice thousands of hours of their time to the cause of bringing you up, making sure you grow into the adult they want you to become. They spent many sleepless nights caring for you as a baby. . .and praying for you as you grew.

Today, thank God for these brave individuals. Ask Him to reward their efforts. And then, once you've finished honoring them in prayer, ask God for the wisdom to be a great parent one day yourself.

THINK ABOUT IT

- How can praying for your parents or guardians increase your appreciation for them?

- Why is it important to pray for your parents even when you don't see eye to eye?

- If you were in their shoes, wouldn't you want someone praying for you?

PRAY ABOUT IT

- Thank God for your parents or guardians, and work on spending more time with them.

- Pay attention to any problems they might face, and bring those problems to God.

- Ask God for the humility to honor them in other ways, including obedience.

Lord, it's easy to sometimes be ungrateful for the ones who are raising me. Bless them for their efforts, and teach me to respect them.

20.
THE MOST IMPORTANT TASK

"Let your light shine in front of men.
Then they will see the good things you do and
will honor your Father Who is in heaven."
MATTHEW 5:16 NLV

Imagine being trained to do a task so important that countless lives counted on its success. Would you move forward on your own, trusting in your own intuition to compensate for your lack of experience? Or would you ask questions, seeking help from the experienced professional who's training you?

Any wise person would choose the latter. But what about when it comes to living for God? Our responsibility as light-bearers in this dark world is the most important task of all, yet it seems many Christians are content with just stumbling through in their own wisdom, hoping time and chance will make their positive impressions outweigh the negative.

But there's a better way. By keeping in constant communication with the God we represent, deepening our relationship with Him and growing in His attributes, we can better display Him to the world.

In order for others to see the light within us, we have to cultivate that light through prayer.

THINK ABOUT IT

- Do you ever pray for God to use your life to reach others?

- How concerned are you with your public image, spiritually speaking?

- How can you share God's light in your friendships with unbelievers?

PRAY ABOUT IT

- Ask God to mold your character into a better representation of His.

- Pray that the right people will enter your life and see God's goodness in you.

- Thank God for the honor of entrusting such a huge responsibility to you.

Father God, help me shine a light on the people in my life—my classmates, friends, family members, and even the strangers I meet in the street.

21.
THE WORD

*In the beginning was the Word, and the Word
was with God, and the Word was God.*
JOHN 1:1 SKJV

The best life is one that's lived with the proper perspective. Think too lowly of yourself and you'll never make an impact. Think too highly and whatever impact you make will be stained by pride.

In building the proper perspective, today's verse is a great place to start. It reminds us that the world didn't begin with us, nor are we the author of this cosmic drama that's unfolding. Jesus was there at the start, long before any of us arrived.

Notice that Jesus is called the "Word." Words are meant for communication, so to whom is God speaking? *Us!* Even though our lives are simply small blips on the radar of eternity, God values us so much that He went out of His way to open a line of communication with us. In return, what else can we do but thank Him. . .and listen to what He has to say?

THINK ABOUT IT

- Why do you think God wants to communicate with us? (See Genesis 1:26.)

- Why don't any of us deserve to speak with God?

- How can we avoid taking this line of communication for granted?

PRAY ABOUT IT

- Ask God to open your eyes to how amazing the act of prayer is.

- Pray with the knowledge that God anticipated your prayer before the world began.

- Thank God for valuing you enough to want to speak with you any time of day.

Lord Jesus, thank You for being the Word that connects us to God, and vice versa. Give me a better understanding of Your infinite love toward me.

22.
HOARDING WISDOM

*I ask God that you may know what He wants
you to do. I ask God to fill you with the wisdom
and understanding the Holy Spirit gives.*
COLOSSIANS 1:9 NLV

You've probably prayed for wisdom for yourself at some point. Maybe it was during a hard test, when the answers just weren't coming to mind. Or maybe you were facing a tough decision and you needed a quick flash of clarity in order to proceed.

Such prayers are admirable, but how often do you pray the same prayers. . .for others? When you hear a friend tell you about a hard choice he's about to make, do you say, "Wow, sounds tough," and then move on? Or do you stop to ask God to reveal the answer to this person as if you were the one making the choice?

Today's prayer proves that the apostle Paul wasn't content with just asking God for wisdom in his own life—he wanted others to benefit from it too. Wisdom isn't something to be hoarded. . .God has an infinite supply.

THINK ABOUT IT

- Have you ever asked for prayer in a tough situation?
- Why do you think God wants as many people as possible to pray for each other?
- What can prayer for other people accomplish? (See James 5:16.)

PRAY ABOUT IT

- Put yourself in the shoes of someone who's having a hard time, and then pray accordingly.
- Pray that God will increase your empathy and reveal ways you can intercede for others.
- Ask God to grant others all the spiritual insights you seek for yourself.

Generous God, thank You for giving wisdom for those who ask. Please intercede in the lives of my friends and family, giving them the wisdom they need to serve You.

23.
SEARCHING FOR SERVICE

*"Do for other people what you would
like to have them do for you."*
LUKE 6:31 NLV

Many Christians subconsciously read this verse in the negative, taking it to mean, "Don't do anything to others you wouldn't have them do to you." But is such a passive life really what God wants for us? Of course not! He doesn't want us to just refrain from treating others poorly—He wants us to go out of our way to treat others with kindness.

Prayer is a great way to jump headlong into this process. By asking God to make you more aware of your role in life (and in the lives of others), you can proceed to make a difference with clear, solid goals in mind. No longer will you have to stumble aimlessly through each day, hoping you don't offend anyone; instead, you'll feel the invigorating freedom of actively living for God, becoming His hands and feet to the ones who need Him most.

THINK ABOUT IT

- What's one new way you can actively fulfill today's verse?

- How willing are you to go out of your way to be the kind of person you'd want in your own life?

- How does the end result of passive living compare to that of an active, goal-driven life?

PRAY ABOUT IT

- Ask God for a passion to serve others—even when it might cost you a lot.

- Pray for selflessness—the ability to see others' needs before your own.

- Pray for God to clarify your purpose in life so that you can go out and live it.

Lord, I want to have action-fueled love for You and everyone I meet. Give me the willingness to search for ways to serve.

24.
STAY AWAKE

Do not let yourselves get tired of doing good.
GALATIANS 6:9 NLV

"Do not let yourselves get tired." What a command! Isn't weariness just a natural human response to constant work? How in the world can we *will* our bodies and minds to avoid feeling tired?

Answer: we can't. In the heat of the moment, it takes something outside of ourselves to increase our mental and spiritual strength. For a good example, think of the last time you stayed up late studying for a test. You probably felt extremely sleepy, so you may have gotten a cup of coffee or stepped out into the cool night air to give your concentration that extra little boost.

Well, prayer is like that. It's a recognition that on your own, you're just not strong enough, and it's a plea for God to give you the extra boost you need to keep pressing on. So whenever you feel the pricking points of spiritual sleepiness in your heart, don't be afraid to ask God to help you stay awake.

THINK ABOUT IT

- How can weariness affect the quality of our spiritual lives?

- How long can Christians persist on their own before caving in to spiritual fatigue?

- What's the hardest part, in your opinion, about staying motivated for God?

PRAY ABOUT IT

- Tell God when you are starting to feel tired in your service to Him.

- Pray not just for the strength to keep going but for the passion to live joyfully for Him.

- Pray for God to remind you why you're living this life in the first place.

I won't lie, Father: the Christian life is tough sometimes. Please grant me the attitude of Paul and Silas in prison—joy and strength, even when despair seems the normal response.

25.
SMILE FOR THE CAMERA

*If we say that we have no sin, we lie to
ourselves and the truth is not in us.*
1 John 1:8 nlv

If you've ever watched amusing videos of "dumb criminals" caught on camera, you've probably seen a variation of this one: the thief walks down the hallway, unaware his every move is being recorded as security footage. When he finally notices the camera, he runs up to the lens, giving the viewer a clear view of his face, and frantically tries to cover the camera before running away.

How often are we like these foolish thieves? Sure, most of us don't rob businesses, but how honest are we in prayer? Do we pray openly about some things. . .but then try covering up the truth when it comes to our sins? Such deception fools nobody but ourselves. God already saw what we did, and any attempt to hide it from Him will be as effective as running up and smiling for the camera.

Why not cut to the chase and be honest?

THINK ABOUT IT

- Most of us know that God is all-knowing, so why do we still try to hide things from Him?

- Why is it a *good* thing that God knows everything about us?

- Why shouldn't the Christian fear being honest with God?

PRAY ABOUT IT

- If there's something you haven't told God, tell Him now.

- Ask God to reveal any sins or harmful attitudes you may not even be aware of.

- Thank Him for the freedom that comes with being able to confess everything.

Father, You already know everything about me, yet You still see me as Your child. Cause my honesty with You to be as complete as Your love toward me.

26.
COME BOLDLY

Let us come boldly to the throne of grace, that we may obtain mercy and find grace to help in time of need.
HEBREWS 4:16 SKJV

Yesterday, we talked about the importance of honesty as it relates to confessing our sins. So what about other topics that don't involve sin. . .but which we may feel embarrassed to bring before God? Maybe you're struggling with anxiety over that class presentation tomorrow, and you feel it'd be foolish to pray about it. After all, God's got bigger things to worry about. Surely, He doesn't want to hear about such a small thing, right?

Wrong! God has adopted us as sons and daughters, and to Him, the title *Father* is far more than a formality. He listens to our every request, no matter how small or seemingly insignificant. He loves it when His children make full use of the privilege of prayer, and He's never annoyed or put off by their cries.

So don't wait to pray until something big comes up—go boldly before God's throne right now.

THINK ABOUT IT

- Are there some things you'd feel embarrassed to pray about? Why or why not?

- How can we reconcile God's infinite power with His intimate love in our minds?

- How can "tiny" prayers be used to build a deeper relationship with God?

PRAY ABOUT IT

- Start speaking with God like you would a friend—don't be afraid of small talk.

- Ask God to make you more comfortable with prayer in every situation.

- Just as you pray for the little things, make sure you thank Him for the little things too.

Thank You, God, for never tiring of my requests. Help me never to be ashamed of spilling my heart out to You.

27.
THE RIGHT START

"Our Father who is in heaven, hallowed be Your name."
MATTHEW 6:9 SKJV

Today's verse marks the beginning of "The Lord's Prayer"—
Jesus' prayer that He modeled for His followers.

Notice that Jesus didn't begin with a request or even
a "thank You." Instead, He started with the one thing that
matters the most: God's holiness and power. Just as a letter
to a friend or family member often begins with the words
dear or *beloved*, Jesus' prayer begins with a recognition of
God's status as the holiest of all. In fact, God's righteousness is the very reason we pray to Him in the first place,
so it only stands to reason that a recognition of this fact
is the perfect starting point.

Doing so requires a humble spirit—a shift of focus
from ourselves and our needs and onto the very reason
we exist: to praise God. By taking care of this step first, we
can put the rest of our prayer into perspective, ensuring
our petitions won't be stained by selfishness.

THINK ABOUT IT

- How can you emphasize God's righteousness and power in your prayers?

- How can we prevent making this part of our prayers just another mindless routine?

- Do you feel genuinely in awe over God's glory? If so, in what ways do your prayers express it?

PRAY ABOUT IT

- Dwell on all the attributes that set God apart from us, and then incorporate your reactions to them into your prayers.

- Ask God to give you a better understanding of who He is.

- Pray for the humility to put His honor above your wants, no matter how strongly you feel toward them.

Lord, You are holy beyond imagination. Your goodness and power are unparalleled in all of creation. Teach me to revere Your name.

28.
THE KINGDOM IS ALREADY HERE

*"Your kingdom come. Your will be done
on earth as it is in heaven."*
MATTHEW 6:10 SKJV

It's easy to read over this part of the Lord's Prayer without considering what it really means. On the surface, it seems to be a broad, somewhat vague desire for God to have His way on earth. But let's look a little closer, starting with the word "kingdom."

In Luke 17:21 (SKJV), Jesus said, "The kingdom of God is within you." And elsewhere, Jesus spoke as if God's kingdom had already arrived and was growing like seeds or bread dough by the action of yeast (Matthew 12:28; 13:31–32, 33). In other words, the "kingdom of God" isn't just a castle in the sky—it consists of *us*. So when we say to God, "Your kingdom come. Your will be done on earth," it's a plea for Him to use us. After all, the church is Jesus' body (1 Corinthians 12:27)—the primary method He uses to carry out His plans.

Whenever you pray for God's will to be done in a situation, don't be shocked if He appoints *you* to be His hands and feet!

THINK ABOUT IT

- When you pray for God to bless someone, how willing are you to "put legs" on those prayers?

- Do you treat your prayers like a partnership with God or just a distant request?

- In what ways can you help God's kingdom flourish in your neighborhood today?

PRAY ABOUT IT

- Ask God to reveal ways you can make a difference.

- Pray for the wisdom to handle the gift of His kingdom in a way that pleases Him.

- Pray for God's desires to become your own.

Lord, I want to be Your hands in a world that needs Your touch. I'm tired of sitting back and watching— it's time to start fighting for Your kingdom.

29.
BASIC NEEDS

"Give us this day our daily bread."
MATTHEW 6:11 SKJV

Many Christians, especially those who follow God for the prosperity they think He'll give them, may be confused by today's prayer. Notice that Jesus didn't say, "Give us this day a million dollars". . .or "Give us unlimited food". . .or "Give us all the pleasure we could ever want." A simple request for "daily bread" is enough.

But why? Isn't God able to give us anything we ask for? Yes, but He also knows that what we ask for is often not the best for us. God knows that earthly pleasures are not the purpose of life—serving Him is. And in order to serve God, all we need is the simple means to live day by day. That new phone or gaming system will bring temporary enjoyment, yes. . .but ultimately, our number one priority is the willingness to use our time and possessions to glorify God.

What are your priorities in prayer?

THINK ABOUT IT

- What are the things you pray for the most?
- When were you last frustrated by unanswered prayer?
- Why might you be grateful if God *doesn't* answer one of your prayers?

PRAY ABOUT IT

- Ask God to give you what you need to effectively serve Him.
- Pray for contentment whenever the things you want seem unobtainable.
- Thank God for all the "unneeded" blessings you do have.

Father God, I don't want to be selfish and ask for things that would benefit only me. Provide for my basic needs, and teach me to pray with the big picture in mind.

30.
CLEARING THE WAY

"And forgive us our debts, as we forgive our debtors."
MATTHEW 6:12 SKJV

In some ways, a grudge is a lot like space junk. What begins as a passing angry thought is soon caught in the orbit of our heart, bound to our souls by the attention we give it.

Soon, other grudges join in orbit, colliding with one another and leaving behind a huge debris field of bitterness. Outside observers no longer see the heart—all they see is a cloud of negativity. And for us, the light of the sun becomes obscured by the darkness whirling around.

Even worse, today's verse implies that if we don't forgive others, our prayers for God to forgive us are useless. (Jesus said so explicitly in verse 15.) Our requests to God become like failed rockets, shredded on the way up by the shrapnel of our own cynical thoughts.

For our prayers to reach heaven, we have to first let God clear out the bitterness in our souls. Only then will our requests be heard by the one who can forgive all.

THINK ABOUT IT

- Why won't God forgive someone who refuses to forgive others?

- Is there unresolved anger lurking somewhere in your heart? If so, how willing are you to remove it today?

- How do the wrongs committed against us compare to the ways we've wronged God?

PRAY ABOUT IT

- Ask God to help you better appreciate His forgiveness so you can rejoice in sharing it with others.

- Ask Him for the desire to make your actions toward others consistent with your prayers for yourself.

- Pray that others will see God's forgiveness in you and therefore seek it for themselves.

Lord, forgive me for sinning against You. . .but first enable me to forgive those who've sinned against me.

31.
PREEMPTIVE PRAYER

*"And do not lead us into temptation,
but deliver us from evil."*
MATTHEW 6:13 SKJV

God has the power to give us strength to resist even the strongest of temptations—there's no doubt about that. But what about when you choose a path, knowing full well that strong temptation will await you somewhere along the way? Will God still give you the power to resist? Well, the answer then becomes a little murky.

Instead of seeking out temptations to prove how strong God's power is (echoing Paul's warning in Romans 6:1), we should pray for the wisdom to find ways around these treacherous pathways. Afraid that movie or show might cause you to stumble? Switch it off. Feel yourself getting angrier in a heated discussion with someone on social media? Take a while to cool off before you type something you'll regret.

And then, when all else fails and you still find yourself facing the beast of your worst inclinations, you can sincerely pray to God, "Deliver me from evil."

THINK ABOUT IT

- Why is preemptive prayer often more important than prayer in the heat of the moment?

- How might your life be different if you prayed regularly for God to lead you in pure paths?

- Is it always possible to avoid temptations? Why or why not?

PRAY ABOUT IT

- Ask God to guide your decisions away from potentially sinful pitfalls.

- Pray for God to set you on high alert for any temptations that might be trying to sneak past your radar.

- When you're tempted to sin, be honest with God about your feelings and ask Him for the strength to make the right choice.

Father, I don't want to walk foolishly into the trap of temptation. Teach me how to avoid it when possible. . .and when it isn't, strengthen my resolve.

32.
LIFE-REFLECTING PRAYER

*"For Yours is the kingdom and the power
and the glory forever. Amen."*
MATTHEW 9:13 SKJV

Today's verse is the final line in the Lord's Prayer. At first glance, it might seem to be an exercise in "Christianese," a string of pious words with no real cohesion or theme to tie them together. All of them are true, but why these particular words instead of others?

Because they accurately summarize the rest of the prayer up to this point. Earlier, we learned that God's *kingdom* is the church—us. We also learned that God has the *power* to give us what we need and protect us from sin. And at the very beginning of this discussion of the Lord's Prayer, we spoke of the importance of admitting God's *glory*. So by telling God, "Yours is the kingdom and the power and the glory forever," we're admitting His lordship over our lives, trusting in His ability to lead, and admitting His righteousness in the face of our imperfections.

Jesus' prayer is not just a ritual to be memorized—it's an entire way of life that should naturally shine forth in our conversations with God.

THINK ABOUT IT

- How can you incorporate these three truths into your prayers each day?

- In what ways should Jesus' words in today's verse impact your life?

- How does your life reflect the Lord's Prayer?

PRAY ABOUT IT

- Ask God to help you find your place and purpose in His kingdom.

- Pray for faith whenever the future seems uncertain or even hopeless.

- Dwell on God's splendor and tell Him how amazed and grateful you are for having Him in your life.

Thank You, Father, for being the ruler of my life—the one who gives me purpose. I surrender everything I love and desire to You.

33.
GOD'S PAINTBRUSH

*"Before you were born, I set you apart as holy.
I chose you to speak to the nations for Me."*
JEREMIAH 1:5 NLV

Maybe there's no purpose to anything. Maybe life is just a series of random accidents. Maybe nothing is planned after all.

If you're like most people, these thoughts have probably crossed your mind. Perhaps they've even begun to take root, sending you spiraling into thoughts of hopelessness. If so, remember this: God's not finished with you yet.

Today's verse proves that God is not content with painting a picture on the fly, doing slapdash work He hopes will work out in the end. No, He plays the long game. Like a skilled artist, He began this universe with the end in mind—and you have the privilege of being right here in the middle of it, helping it unfold, brushstroke by brushstroke.

That's why constant communication with God is so important—it sets you in tune with the rhythms of His paintbrush, driving away any thoughts that it all might be in vain.

THINK ABOUT IT

- Today's verse says God chooses our destinies. How is this compatible with our free will?

- How might God's knowledge of a person's future choices impact how He uses that person? How should this affect your prayers for today?

- Why is it futile to try to figure out the whole picture of your life?

PRAY ABOUT IT

- Ask God for the peace to accept life as it comes.

- Pray for the willingness to follow God's nudging, wherever it may lead.

- Thank God for caring enough to plan out your life in advance.

Lord, You know my future better than I know my past. Teach me to anticipate each moment, not as a risk of failure but as an opportunity to continue Your plan.

34.
ENCOURAGING YOURSELF

And David was greatly distressed, for the people spoke of stoning him. . . . But David encouraged himself in the LORD his God.
1 SAMUEL 30:6 SKJV

The only thing worse than a painful death is a life that's lived without God. David understood this truth, so when an angry mob was ready to start chucking rocks at him, his first thought wasn't self-preservation but rather prayer and meditation on God's goodness in his life. Even if he died, God would always be enough for him, now and forever.

What about you? Hopefully you're not facing certain death at the hands of a murderous rabble. But what about when your friends shun you for your faith? When you get nasty looks and cruel comments for refusing to join them in sin? Will you cave into the pressure, sink into despair, or strike up a conversation with the God who offers unlimited peace?

No matter how cut off you feel, you don't have to go it alone. It's never a bad time to encourage yourself in the Lord.

THINK ABOUT IT

- What's your reaction to stressful situations?
- How can you work on making prayer your go-to response when fear crops up?
- How can the mere act of prayer often be encouraging enough?

PRAY ABOUT IT

- Don't wait until the stress becomes unbearable—pray right away.
- Ask God for peace each time you see a stressful situation on the horizon.
- Talk to God like you would a friend, admitting your fears and reminding yourself of His power.

Lord, thank You for always being strong enough to quiet the storms within. Teach me to run to You for shelter rather than trying to brave the elements alone.

35.
GRACE IS FREE, NOT CHEAP

My little children, I write these things to you, that you may not sin. And if any man sins, we have an advocate with the Father, Jesus Christ the righteous.
1 JOHN 2:1 SKJV

There are three types of Christians: those who read the first half of today's verse and ignore the second, those who read the second half and ignore the first, and those who incorporate both halves into their lives equally.

The first group generally rejoices in legalistic behavior, showing no mercy to struggling Christians and driving them further from the church. Their hearts are filled with guilt and an increasingly frantic desire to perfect themselves before God disowns them altogether. The second group of people foolishly plan out their prayers for forgiveness in anticipation of sinning—using repentance like a credit card for a planned purchase. The third group, however, recognizes the importance of preemptive holiness—a firm resolve to keep God's commandments—while also basking in the joy of forgiveness whenever such plans fail.

Which kind of person are you?

THINK ABOUT IT

- How can a Christian teen focus on both halves of today's verse?

- Do you see prayer as an excuse to sin or as a way to avoid it?

- If God can forgive any sin we commit, why do you think He wants us to pray for the strength to avoid it?

PRAY ABOUT IT

- Ask God for the desire to please Him at all times.

- Confess any sins that may still linger in the back of your soul.

- Thank God for the gift of sin-canceling prayer.

Lord, I'm grateful for Your forgiveness, but I never want to treat Your grace like it's cheap. Teach me to understand what it cost You to provide it.

36.
BE AN INFLUENCER

Let no one show little respect for you because you are young. Show other Christians how to live by your life.
1 TIMOTHY 4:12 NLV

Ever notice how youth-driven our culture is? Most advertisements are targeted directly toward teens and young adults, and even the ads that aren't are primarily focused on ways to make older people feel young again.

As a result, today's verse might seem a little out of touch. Young people aren't generally looked down upon anymore. But this new cultural norm makes the verse's message even more powerful: *you have a voice, so use it wisely.*

With every word you speak and every action you take, people are watching. You have the ability to influence your peers, thus making an impact on your rising generation.

When faced with such an overwhelming responsibility, prayer is the best response. Don't be content with fumbling your way through life, unaware of the impressions you're leaving; instead, pray for God to guide your steps so they will become good markers for others to follow.

It's never too early to be a leader.

THINK ABOUT IT

- How much do the opinions of other teens matter to you? How might yours matter to them?

- In what ways are you leading by example?

- When was the last time you prayed for God to use your voice to proclaim His words?

PRAY ABOUT IT

- Ask God for self-awareness when it comes to your moral behavior.

- Pray that out of all the voices in the world, your voice would be something worth listening to.

- Thank God for your uniquely influential position in today's culture.

Lord, may my voice and behavior echo Yours, leading those who see and hear them to You.

37.
FIGHT!

*But avoid foolish questions and genealogies
and contentions and strivings about the law,
for they are unprofitable and vain.*
TITUS 3:9 SKJV

Today's verse provides great guidance for our everyday living. Arguments can crop up anywhere—at home, school, or even with total strangers on the Internet. It seems that friendly discourse is a dead art, replaced with outbursts of emotion.

That's why God wants us to pray for His love to fill our hearts. Without His Spirit of compassion, we'll start seeing people as enemies—visual representations of the opinions we hate. And when everyone else is reduced to little more than a punching bag, how will it be possible to shine the light of God's love?

Today, ask God to help you see the humanity in others, even when you disagree with what they say. Don't fuel the fires of hate and mistrust—pray for a more peaceful world, and then go out and make that world a reality.

THINK ABOUT IT

- Why is the outcome of an argument seldom more important than the way you handle the argument itself?

- How effective is waiting until tempers flare to pray for peace?

- How can you be merciful and kind to others, even when conflict is inevitable?

PRAY ABOUT IT

- Ask God for the patience to wait your turn during a disagreement.

- Ask God for the grace to see the other person's point of view.

- Pray that when an argument is necessary, both parties will walk away in peace.

Father, I'm glad You don't fly off the handle every time I make mistakes. Teach me to show the same degree of love toward those who upset me.

38.
PRAYER WARRIOR

Remember to pray for all Christians.
EPHESIANS 6:18 NLV

Does today's verse mean we should learn the names of every Christian on earth and then cycle through the list? Or does it mean we should simply offer up a quick umbrella prayer for "Christians everywhere"?

As always, the truth lies somewhere in between. Obviously, you'll never learn the names of every Christian, but you do probably know a bunch. Even if you've never met them, you've likely heard of hundreds or even thousands of brothers and sisters in Christ who are facing trials of some sort.

So what should you do when you hear of such a situation? That's right—pray. Don't wait until the name slips from memory; instead, make a habit of sending up a quick prayer for the people you'd otherwise never hear of. And for those whose lives you *are* more familiar with, pray longer and with increased regularity.

Prayer isn't just a nice gesture—it's a powerful tool that can call down God's healing and peace. . .as well as make you more compassionate toward the ones you're praying for.

THINK ABOUT IT

- How well do you pay attention to the prayer requests at your church?

- When was the last time you prayed for a total stranger?

- How would you feel if you knew someone across the globe was praying for you right now?

PRAY ABOUT IT

- Ask God to increase your awareness of Christians who need your prayers.

- Pray for God's will to be done in the lives of those whose situations you don't understand.

- Make a list of the most urgent requests and pray for them each day.

Lord, I want to join Your army of prayer warriors. Teach me how to pray with intentionality and genuine care.

39.
RIGHTEOUS PRAYERS

"But I have prayed for you. I have prayed that your faith will be strong and that you will not give up."
LUKE 22:32 NLV

It's an amazing thing to hear that Jesus prays for His followers. The Son of God—the second person of the Trinity—is interceding with the Father for you!

But what about your own prayers? When others hear that you're praying for them, are they thrilled to know it? Obviously, nobody will ever be as holy as Jesus, but isn't it nice to hear that someone who's close to God is praying for you? Wouldn't you like to be that person for someone else?

James 5:16 teaches that righteousness *does* make a difference when it comes to the impact of our prayers, so we'd do well to amplify our requests with our lifestyle.

Never underestimate the value of a strong relationship with God—it can change your life and the lives of others.

THINK ABOUT IT

- What might you need to change so that your life is consistent with your prayers?

- How well does your life—and your praying—reflect Jesus'?

- What does the fact that Jesus prays for us say about the importance of prayer?

PRAY ABOUT IT

- Thank Jesus for praying for your spiritual well-being.

- Ask God to enable you to pray effectively for others.

- Pray for a stronger relationship with Him, and therefore a stronger prayer life.

Lord Jesus, I'm grateful for the prayers You offer to the Father on my behalf. Help me to be an effective prayer warrior for the people in my life.

40.
BUDDY SYSTEM

Keep awake! Watch at all times. The devil is working against you. He is walking around like a hungry lion with his mouth open. He is looking for someone to eat.
1 Peter 5:8 nlv

In an unfamiliar area, it's nice to have a "buddy system" in place—a friend who accompanies you both for protection and for letting you know if something doesn't seem quite right.

Our spiritual lives are no different. On our own, we're sitting ducks—easy prey for Satan to pick off one by one. We'd never last a day out in the wild by ourselves. But whenever we stay in close contact with God, two things happen: (1) we are protected by a greater power—the Holy Spirit—who lives inside us, and (2) we can become better informed of where potential dangers might be located. By praying for wisdom and discernment, we'll gradually learn which areas and situations to avoid so as not to find ourselves face-to-face with the "hungry lion" of temptation.

Prayer is the most effective "buddy system" of them all. Are you using it?

THINK ABOUT IT

- When did you last make an unwise decision you later wished you would have prayed about?

- How alert are you when it comes to temptation?

- How regularly do you pray for God to reveal the devil's schemes to you?

PRAY ABOUT IT

- Ask God for the insight to stay one step ahead of Satan's plans.

- Pray that God would foil any schemes you don't even know about.

- Pray for God's strength to make up for your weakness when temptation comes.

Lord, I never want to go anywhere without You by my side. Thank You for offering the greatest protection of all.

41.
SHARPEN UP

*Iron is made sharp with iron, and one
man is made sharp by a friend.*
PROVERBS 27:17 NLV

Today's verse uses a striking metaphor to describe how important friendships can be. Without someone to bring out our best qualities and help us fight our worst, even the strongest among us will soon lapse into selfishness and reject accountability.

Prayer is a vital instrument we can use to find these sorts of friendships and keep them alive. God knows, for instance, which friends will benefit you and which ones will only inhibit your spiritual growth. So don't hesitate to ask Him for a soul-sharpening friend—He's more than capable of sending one your way.

Great friendships include more than mere conversation—they feature sincere prayers offered up on each other's behalf. Prayer is a fantastic way of deepening your connection with someone else. By praying for that person's needs, you are showing empathy toward his struggles. Friends, after all, don't pass up opportunities to pray for friends.

THINK ABOUT IT

- How regularly do you pray for your friends? Do they pray for you?

- Do you ask God for wisdom in choosing your friends?

- What will become of a prayerless friendship? Why?

PRAY ABOUT IT

- Thank God for the friends He's placed in your life.

- Listen to your friends' problems and bring them to God each day in prayer.

- Pray that you'll be the kind of friend you'd want to have for yourself.

Lord, I want prayer to color all my relationships and friendships. Teach me how to sharpen others as they sharpen me.

42.
SWEET-SMELLING PRAYERS

The four beasts and twenty-four elders fell down before the Lamb, every one of them having harps and golden vials full of incense, which are the prayers of saints.
REVELATION 5:8 SKJV

Do you ever feel like your prayers have a fear of heights—like as soon as they leave your mouth, they plummet straight to earth with a disappointing thud?

Don't worry, everyone has felt that way. Even Jesus cried out, "My God, My God, why have You forsaken Me?" (Matthew 27:46 SKJV) during His crucifixion. But before you take these discouraging feelings to heart, remember the promises held in today's verse: God keeps your prayers stored safely away in heaven. . .and not only that, but they are also a type of incense to Him—something that brings Him joy.

As a result, each prayer you pray is invaluable, no matter how short, desperate, or disjointed it may be. When you pray, pray with the knowledge that every word you say is being recorded up above, ready to be answered when the time is right.

THINK ABOUT IT

- Why do you think God is sometimes "silent" when we pray?

- What would happen to your spiritual and emotional health if you received everything you prayed for right away? Why?

- Which long-abandoned prayers might you need to dig up and start praying again?

PRAY ABOUT IT

- Be persistent in your prayers, knowing God loves to hear from you.

- Try to imagine God physically before you, then talk to Him like you would an old friend who's thrilled to see you.

- Ask God to align your prayers and desires with the things He wants in your life.

Lord, even when it feels like You aren't listening, I know You are. Thank You for keeping track of my many requests.

43.
NO PRIDE WHERE PRAISE IS

*God has given me His loving-favor. This helps me
write these things to you. I ask each one of you not
to think more of himself than he should think.*
ROMANS 12:3 NLV

What is humility? Is it denying your talents and pretending
you're no good at something? No—that's false modesty.
Is it belittling yourself until even you start to agree with
your insults? No—that's self-loathing. So what is it?

Well, as pastor and author Rick Warren once said,
"True humility is not thinking less of yourself; it is thinking
of yourself less." The moment you turn all your attention
toward making yourself appear humble is the moment
you've suddenly become prideful. Humility is less of a skill
than it is a natural result of a proper understanding of God.

The best way to gain this understanding is to spend
time in His Word and in prayer. When you have frequent
conversations with God, all thoughts of yourself and your
own importance will fade away in light of the awe and
reverence you feel for His power and goodness.

Humility isn't learned overnight—it's gained through
frequent exposure to the infinite God you serve.

THINK ABOUT IT

- Why does learning more about God inevitably lead to praise?

- Why is pride incompatible with praise?

- When was the last time you sincerely praised God?

PRAY ABOUT IT

- Ask God to turn your attention so high that it reaches over your head and sees only Him.

- Thank God for revealing parts of His infinite majesty to us finite humans.

- Pray for a better understanding of God's attributes.

God, I'm overwhelmed by the sheer scale of Your glory. Help me to focus on that—not on my own limited skills.

44.
PRAISE WARM-UPS

A voice came from the throne, saying,
"Give thanks to our God, you servants
who are owned by Him. Give thanks to
our God, you who honor Him with love
and fear, both small and great."
REVELATION 19:5 NLV

Professional singers perform vocal warm-ups before a show—short exercises designed to relax their muscles and vocal cords. Once these exercises are taken care of, the real show can begin, and the singers are free to use the full range of their talents to impress the crowd.

In a spiritual sense, all our praise here on earth is a warm-up for the eternal song we're preparing to sing in heaven. Right now, true praise is often difficult because our minds are clouded by the evil and pain we see. But in heaven, we'll see God only—and continually be in His presence for all eternity. Each new second will be as thrilling as the one that came before, and praise will issue from our lips like a beautiful song.

Are you ready for that day?

THINK ABOUT IT

- How can you incorporate praise consistently in your prayers?
- Do you feel obligated to praise God, or does your praise flow from your heart?
- What forms can praise take in prayer and everyday life?

PRAY ABOUT IT

- Dwell on the events of the day and praise God for each one.
- Praise God for walking beside you in this dark world.
- Praise God for the hope that waits for you in heaven.

Lord, teach me to praise You from the heart each day. I can't wait for that eternal day of praise that's coming.

45.
PLEAD THEIR CASE

*And Abraham. . .said, "Will You also destroy the
righteous with the wicked? Perhaps there are fifty
righteous within the city. Will You also destroy and not
spare the place for the fifty righteous who are in it?"*
Genesis 18:23–24 skjv

In the verses following today's passage, Abraham pled
fervently with God to spare the wicked cities of Sodom
and Gomorrah from destruction. Eventually, God agreed to
hold back His judgment if He found ten righteous people
in the cities. Sadly, that did not happen.

One key takeaway from this passage is that Abraham
begged God as if his own life were in danger. His pleas
were so desperate that, taken out of context, one might
assume he himself lived in one of these cities!

That's how we should act in our prayers—just as
eager to see God intervene in another person's life as we
are to see Him intervene in our own. We're all made in
God's image, so any blessings one person receives should
be felt by us all.

This is what intercession is all about. And it's something God calls each of us to do.

THINK ABOUT IT

- What's wrong with gloating over a bad person's punishment?

- Do you spend as much time praying for others as you do for yourself?

- What role does empathy play in prayer? How can you work on building it up?

PRAY ABOUT IT

- Pray for God to have mercy on those who still have a chance to repent.

- Thank Him for sparing you when you deserved nothing but death.

- Ask God for the empathy to sincerely plead another person's case before Him.

Lord, please save my lost friends and family members. I don't want them to die in their sins. I was just like them once, and I want nothing more than to see them come to You.

46.
DESPERATE TIMES. . .

And they struck them with the edge of the
sword. . . . And they brought out the images from
the house of Baal and burned them. And they
broke down the image of Baal and broke down the
house of Baal and made it a latrine to this day.
2 KINGS 10:25–27 SKJV

King Jehu wasn't content with letting pagan priests off
with a slap on the wrist—desperate times called for desperate measures.

Today, God doesn't call us to round up pagans and start
hacking. But what about the false gods in our hearts? Our
bodies are temples of the Holy Spirit (1 Corinthians 6:19),
but that doesn't mean that idols—things that replace our
devotion to God—won't creep through the windows from
time to time.

That's why constant prayer is necessary in the life
of a Christian teen. Conversing often with your Creator
is a great way to keep yourself from slipping into idola-
trous behaviors. Today, ask God to help you round up any
ungodly affections that may have crept into your heart. . .
and then start chopping.

THINK ABOUT IT

- What would have happened had Jehu let some idol worshiping slide?

- In what ways are you as serious about idols as Jehu?

- What are some idols that creep into the lives of modern Christians? Can you spot any in your life?

PRAY ABOUT IT

- Ask God to make you ruthless in your hunt for false affections in your heart.

- Pray for the strength to let go of anything that might become an idol.

- Pray for God to renew your dedication to Him each day.

Lord, I never want anything—no matter how innocent it is by itself—to replace You in my life. Help me eliminate all idols today.

47.
MISSION: POSSIBLE

It is written, "Be holy, for I am holy."
1 PETER 1:16 SKJV

In the list of impossible biblical commands, today's verse seems to take the gold medal. After all, how are we sinful humans supposed to compare with God's righteousness? Aren't we already doomed the moment we commit our first sin?

Yes, but that's why God offers us ways we can become holy. The first and most obvious way is via salvation. Jesus' death on the cross and our acceptance of it took away our guilt and made us just as holy as He is, like we've never even sinned. Second, God sends His Holy Spirit into our souls to guide us into a life of increased holiness—a process called *sanctification*. If repentance is an antidote for sin, then sanctification is the medicine you take to avoid getting sick.

Both methods are inseparably linked to prayer—the act of coming to God in humility, acknowledging your mistakes and weaknesses, and asking Him to mold you into His image. So today, pray for holiness and watch as God does what He does best.

THINK ABOUT IT

- Is it possible for humans to achieve holiness by themselves?

- How often do you pray for God to improve your behaviors and thoughts?

- How has the process of sanctification changed your life?

PRAY ABOUT IT

- Thank God for applying His righteousness to you.

- Pray that you'll never give up on your journey toward meeting God's standard.

- Ask God for the strength to get back up again whenever you trip.

Lord, only You are naturally holy. . .but because of my faith in You, I now share in this holiness. Help me to never treat this gift with contempt.

48.
RESCUE THE PERISHING

*My prayer to God is that the Jews might be
saved from the punishment of sin.*
ROMANS 10:1 NLV

Even if you're the kind of teen who doesn't go out much
or is homeschooled, you probably know at least a dozen
people who haven't accepted Jesus as Lord. And if you're
an extrovert or attend a public school, well. . .that number
might be in the hundreds.

The point is, there's no shortage of lost people in the
world—a sad fact that only grows sadder with each new
teen or young adult who leaves the church. So what are
you to do? Stay paralyzed with fear? Hide your faith? Join
their ranks? No. There are two appropriate responses for
Christian teens who find themselves swimming in a sea
of sinners: (1) be the light these people would otherwise
never see, and (2) pray like your own soul depends on it.

Bring as many names as you can before God each day,
trusting that He'll listen and intervene in their lives. Who
knows? Maybe it's your prayer that will tip the scales and
cause someone to finally see the light.

THINK ABOUT IT

- How many lost people do you know?

- How often do you pray for them?

- If you didn't know God, wouldn't you like for someone to pray for your salvation?

PRAY ABOUT IT

- Ask God to help you care more about lost souls.

- Pray that your words and actions will point someone toward God today.

- Pray for an increased awareness of the lost people around you today.

Lord, the number of lost people in the world is overwhelming sometimes. Help me to go out and represent your kingdom anyway, bringing as many as I can to You.

49.
IN JESUS' NAME

*"Until now you have not asked for anything
in My name. Ask and you will receive."*
JOHN 16:24 NLV

"In Jesus' name, amen."

How many times have you heard or spoken those words? There's nothing wrong with ending your prayers like this, of course. But is simply saying this phrase enough to fulfill Jesus' command?

Asking for something in Jesus' name isn't just saying words—it's a recognition that Jesus is the mediator between you and the Father, as well as the acknowledgment that the content and tone of your prayer is something Jesus would approve. Praying, "Give me what I want, whether You want me to have it or not", and adding the words "In Jesus' name" at the end is just another way of taking His name in vain.

In other words, don't let the act of praying in Jesus' name become a thoughtless epilogue to your requests—rather, let it influence the direction of your prayers, and comfort you with the fact that Jesus is mediating for You as you speak.

THINK ABOUT IT

- Why do we pray in Jesus' name?

- How can you avoid praying for things that Jesus would not approve of?

- What are some ways you can prevent this command from becoming routine?

PRAY ABOUT IT

- Pray for God to align your prayers with Jesus' will for your life.

- Ask God for a better understanding of Jesus' role as the mediator in your prayers.

- When you talk with God, pray as if Jesus is right there with you (because He is!).

Father, may my requests always be worthy of the name in which I make them. Teach me to use Jesus' name reverently at all times.

50.
DEAFENING SILENCE

And this is the confidence that we have in Him, that if we ask anything according to His will, He hears us.
1 John 5:14 skjv

A lot of former Christians have walked away from the faith because of "unanswered" prayer. Maybe it was a sick relative or friend who passed away, a relationship that failed, or even an injury that refused to heal.

If you've ever been in a situation like that, you know how deafening God's apparent silence can be. But today's verse is here to assure you that God *does* hear. He understands your worry when your friend is rushed to the hospital. He feels your hurt when that breakup leaves you emotionally drained. And He knows your pain when you just feel empty inside, like there's nothing worth living for anymore.

He knows. . .and as long as you stay by Him, He's willing to lead you through to the joy that waits for you on the other side of your anguish.

THINK ABOUT IT

- How can you make sure your requests align with God's will?

- Why does God allow disappointments even when we pray for them not to happen?

- How can the promise of heaven ease our pain during temporary tragedies?

PRAY ABOUT IT

- Ask God for His will to be done, even if His will causes pain for today.

- Pray for the patience to endure suffering and the wisdom to understand it's for a reason.

- Pray that you'll never grow cynical when you don't get the answer you want.

All-knowing Lord, please have Your way in my life. I surrender all my desires and plans to You. Change or break them as You please. I know Your plan will be far, far better.

51.
PATIENCE IS A VIRTUE

*Tribulation works patience, and patience
experience, and experience hope.*
ROMANS 5:3–4 SKJV

Imagine a high-rise for Christian virtues. On the first few floors are specific virtues like honesty, chastity, and temperance. All are vitally important, of course, but usually under the control of the ones on the middle floors: virtues like integrity, humility, and so on. And then there's the penthouse virtues—the fundamental forces driving the Christian life: qualities like love, faith, hope. . .and patience.

Yes, patience is right there at the top of the list. Why? Because of how deeply entrenched it needs to be in our lives. From waiting in line at the grocery store to waiting on Jesus' return, your entire life is a trial of patience. Faith itself is really another form of patience—waiting on God for answers you can't see. And today's verse says that hope—one of the "Big Three" (1 Corinthians 13:13)—finds its source in patience.

So today, if you pray for anything, pray for patience. But be warned: it can only be gained through the trials that produce it—and God may just give it to you when you ask.

THINK ABOUT IT

- How often do pray for patience?

- In what areas of your life does your patience shine the strongest?

- Can a person ever reach the point in which prayers for patience are no longer needed?

PRAY ABOUT IT

- Ask God to give you His eternal perspective.

- Pray that you'll be as patient with others as He is with you.

- Pray for the strength to be patient in small things as practice for the things that matter.

No matter what it takes, God, I'm willing to learn patience. Strengthen my soul so I'm able to endure the lessons.

52.
NO TIME LIKE THE PRESENT

Now is the day of salvation.
2 Corinthians 6:2 skjv

Yesterday, we learned how important it is to gain patience and other virtues—and how the best way to grow these fruits is by watering your life with constant prayer. But merely making vague requests for God to improve your life isn't enough. You've got to stay on the lookout for weaknesses, hone in on whatever you find, and ask God to help you start improving *today*. Don't be like Augustine in his early years, praying to God, "Give me chastity and temperance—but not yet!"

Many Christian teens give the future too much credit, viewing it as a magical place where all their plans for self-improvement abide. But the tricky thing about the future is that it never arrives. There will always only be *now*.

When you pray for virtues, don't be content to shove them into an ever-dwindling future. Instead, pray in the present tense, always prepared to follow God's ongoing process of sanctification.

THINK ABOUT IT

- What weaknesses do you need to work on *today*?

- How are you praying for God to work in your life right now, as opposed to "someday"?

- Why is procrastination one of the deadliest faults of all?

PRAY ABOUT IT

- Ask God to fill you with a sense of immediacy about your spiritual well-being.

- Whatever you need to improve, pray for the chance to begin right now.

- Pray for God to help you live in the present, taking your walk with Him one day at a time.

Lord, I know my future with You is bright but only if I follow Your light today. Teach me never to put off serving You.

53.
THE WHOLE TRUTH

*"If you continue in My word, then you are
My disciples indeed. And you shall know the
truth, and the truth shall make you free."*
JOHN 8:31–32 SKJV

"The truth is out there."

Ever heard this phrase? It was used in the sci-fi tele-vision show *The X-Files*, and ever since, it's become a tag-line for conspiracy theorists everywhere—a mantra that reinforces the belief that if a person digs long enough, the truth will be found.

Fortunately, Jesus has a much better system for dis-covering truth—abiding in Him. We don't have to trek to Area 51 or infiltrate the CIA to find what we need to know—all we have to do is stay by Jesus' side, praying and reading God's Word.

Want to know how to respond to a situation? Ask God and then look for clues in the Bible, trusting that He'll reveal it to you (James 1:5).

The truth isn't out there somewhere—it's right here, waiting to be gleaned today.

THINK ABOUT IT

- How can prayer help ease the searching soul?

- In what ways have you been frustrated by your quest for spiritual truth?

- Why do you think God expects us to ask for the truth—as opposed to Him just giving it to us?

PRAY ABOUT IT

- Ask God to help you rely on Him as your sole source of spiritual knowledge.

- When you're stumped by a problem, pray for the wisdom to work through it in a Christ-like way.

- Pray for insight each time you read the Bible.

Thank You, Jesus, for having all the answers.
May I never pursue truth in places that
can only offer lies and deception.

54.
HEART DEMOLITION

*Make a clean heart in me, O God. Give me
a new spirit that will not be moved.*
PSALM 51:10 NLV

Notice that in today's verse, the psalmist isn't asking God to work with preexisting materials. No, his prayer is much more radical. He asks God to create an entirely new heart to replace the old one. He doesn't need a home renovator—he needs a wrecking ball and an architect who knows what He's doing.

Left to our own devices, each one of our hearts can start looking like a house in an episode of *Hoarders*—gross and messy. But once we make that step and ask God to tear the place down and start afresh, our filthy hearts are soon transformed into shining mansions of holiness. And if we ever find ourselves starting to hoard again—gathering up dirty boxes of sin and stashing them in the corner—God is always here to perform a clean sweep of forgiveness and renew our passion for righteousness whenever we ask.

You don't have to settle for a heart that's cluttered with shame and regret. Ask God for a fresh, clean start today.

THINK ABOUT IT

- In what ways is your heart in need of a clean-up. . .or a demolition followed by a fresh new start?

- Why aren't we able to clean our hearts without God?

- What role does the Holy Spirit play in making our hearts clean?

PRAY ABOUT IT

- Ask God to make you aware of how clean or dirty your heart is.

- Pray for the willingness to let Him do His work whenever things get too cluttered inside.

- Thank Him for His free "construction" and "housecleaning" services.

Father, You're the master designer, so You know exactly how my heart should look. Make it something new today.

55.
GRIMY BUSINESS TACTICS

But put on the Lord Jesus Christ, and do not make provision for the flesh, to fulfill its lusts.
ROMANS 13:14 SKJV

Temptation is like a crooked salesperson, always promising a great deal but leaving you with a product you wish you'd never bought.

The devil wrote the book on slippery slopes. He knocks politely at the door, saying things like, "Just one look won't hurt" or "It's just a white lie." And then, once he's slipped inside, he'll blow your life apart from the inside like a stick of dynamite. The only way to protect yourself from this dangerous foe is to "put on the Lord Jesus Christ." And one of the best ways to do that is to pray—as hard and as often as you can.

Your battle against the devil isn't a friendly tennis match—it's a war. From the images on your phone to the "harmless" chatter of your friends at school, Satan is constantly devising situations to tempt you to fall. You can't outwit him, and no matter how hard you try, his attacks *will* wear you down if you go it alone.

With Jesus' help, however, victory is guaranteed.

THINK ABOUT IT

- How often do you struggle with repeated sin?

- How often do you let your guard down when it comes to "small" sins?

- How often do you incorporate prayer into your battles against temptation?

PRAY ABOUT IT

- Pray for the wisdom to spot a bad deal when you see it.

- Ask God to help you be uncompromising in your standards.

- Pray for the strength to resist sin, even the kind that seems impossibly alluring.

Sin is a powerful force, God—but Your power triumphs over all. Teach me to tap into Your strength.

56.
BEING A FRIEND

Draw near to God and He will draw near to you.
JAMES 4:8 SKJV

Imagine you have a girlfriend you never talk to. No calls, no texts, no face-to-face conversations—nothing to keep the relationship alive. And yet you act as if you're thriving together. You have a picture of her in your bedroom, a collection of letters she sent you (to which you never responded), and even a custom-made shirt with her name emblazoned on it. Everyone who knows you knows how much you value your girlfriend—everyone except your girlfriend.

Pretty absurd, right? Well, that's exactly what it's like for a "Christian" who never prays. Salvation isn't a set of rules—it's a relationship with the Savior who died for you. If you don't treat that relationship as important, you might as well toss out all the associated gear, your crosses and vaguely inspirational T-shirts. Without a relationship, they're just empty items, taking up space everywhere except for where it counts: your heart.

Draw near to God today by having a heartfelt conversation with your Creator.

THINK ABOUT IT

- Do you treat God like a word or idea, or do you treat Him like a friend?

- Is there a limit to what kinds of prayer can deepen your relationship with God?

- Are you actively trying to draw closer to Him today?

PRAY ABOUT IT

- Tell God what's on your heart and listen for His reply.

- Ask God to help you be less ritualistic and more personal when it comes to your spiritual life.

- Pray that your journey toward God never reaches a point of stagnation or apathy.

You're the best friend I could ever ask for, Lord, so I want to be a friend in return.

57.
WORTHLESS THINGS

Turn my eyes away from looking at what is worthless, and revive me in Your way.
PSALM 119:37 SKJV

In this life, there are plenty of "worthless" things vying for a Christian guy's attention. Everything from drug use to pornography to rebellious role models shine like neon lights in a sleepless city, beckoning the passerby to partake in their forbidden pleasures. And the longer you gaze into the glow, the more likely you'll find yourself entranced. Soon, your legs will unconsciously walk in that direction.

Look away! Don't focus your attention on the worthless attitudes and behaviors of those around you—nothing is there but hopelessness, disappointment, and (if you look too long) a soul-killing trap. Instead, tether yourself to prayer so you are always facing God's love—the brightness of which far outshines sin's artificial glow. Come to God every day for strength in filtering out the lights of the city. And when you feel yourself distracted by the deadening tug of godlessness, call out to God to reel you back in.

THINK ABOUT IT

- What are some of the "worthless" things that people your age idolize?

- Have you become distracted by a "worthless" thing?

- When a mind is divided between God and sin, why do you think it always ends up choosing sin?

PRAY ABOUT IT

- Pray that God's truth will always hold priority in your mind over sin's lies.

- Practice praying each time you feel your mind start drifting toward forbidden thoughts and desires.

- Tell God every time you're tempted and ask Him to fix your eyes on Him alone.

Father, keep my mind off worthless things and on the most valuable treasure in the world: You.

58.
CARNAL MINDS

The carnal mind is enmity against God, for it is not subject to the law of God nor indeed can be.
ROMANS 8:7 SKJV

It's easy enough to be a law-abiding citizen. Don't throw bricks at storefront windows. Don't set the woods on fire. Don't hurt people. Don't (if you have a driver's license) go eighty miles an hour in a forty-five zone. And, whatever you do, don't tear the tags off mattresses! (Okay, that last one might be a joke.)

But what about when it comes to God's law? Well, today's verse says that any of us who are living "carnally"—in the flesh—simply cannot obey God the way we should. Why? Because our fallen human nature is fundamentally incompatible with the standard God has set. To live out His commands takes the power of the Holy Spirit—and even then, you still have to put forth the effort to ask for it.

So never feel like it's a sign of weakness to pray, and never view prayer as a last resort. It's the only shot you have at making sure your life is pleasing to God.

THINK ABOUT IT

- Why are God's grace and flagrant, willing sin incompatible?

- How can a Christian work toward killing off the carnal mind?

- How often do you pray to have a Spirit-filled mind instead of a carnal one?

PRAY ABOUT IT

- Pray for a godly mindset—one that's driven by the Spirit and not selfishness.

- Admit to God that you can't obey Him on your own.

- Confess your sins and ask God to help you learn from your mistakes.

Thank You, Lord, for refusing to leave me powerless in my struggle against sin. Help me leave my carnal mind behind and replace it with Your spiritual power.

59.
ONE THING REMAINS

"Heaven and earth will pass away,
but My words will not pass away."
MATTHEW 24:35 NLV

Think for a moment of the end of time. The earth, the cosmos, and every element within them are dissolving into nothingness. Every physical thing that once gave humanity a sense of purpose is suddenly evaporating. The only thing that remains is the Word.

Most Christians believe this, so why do many of us behave like we don't? Our eternal Savior sacrificed Himself so we may survive the death of all things and be with Him forever. Why do we feel embarrassed or unwilling to stay in His presence today? Our prayers should be seasoned with gratitude and reverence, yet for many of us, they've been turned into little more than rituals to be endured rather than privileges to be used. He holds the key to the meaning of life, yet we're often too busy looking for purpose elsewhere.

Today, when you pray, be attentive to any answers God might provide. After all, His words are the only things that will last forever.

THINK ABOUT IT

- Why do you think so many people put their faith in short-lived pleasures?

- How can a Christian teen stay focused on eternal things over the temporary?

- In what way do you treat God's words like the valuable treasures they are?

PRAY ABOUT IT

- Pray for God to reveal the meaning of His words when you read the Bible.

- Thank God for caring enough to give us His eternal words.

- Ask Him for the desire to find all your answers in Jesus.

Lord, I don't want to chase temporary things, even if these things have the loudest voice. Teach me to hear Your true whisper above the world's lying shout.

60.
THE FINAL STRETCH

Look to yourselves, that we don't lose those things that we have worked for, but that we receive a full reward.
2 John 8 skjv

Imagine participating in an Olympic race. You're in first place, everyone else is far behind you, and you're rounding the final turn. You feel pride surge through your body as you look up from the track at the countless cheering fans all around you. You flash a smile, head held high—so high, in fact, that you lose your rhythm. You trip, spraining your ankle, and the runners in second, third, and fourth speed past you at the final second. You hobble across the line, but it's too late. Victory was right there, but your pride caused you to blow it.

That's the warning today's verse provides. In order to avoid such a fall, we must stay in constant prayer, keeping our spiritual rhythm as we listen for God's instructions. The moment we try to go it alone—even if we're in the final stretch—is the moment our stumble is guaranteed.

Today, don't lose all you've worked for. Stay in contact with God, and He'll make sure all your efforts succeed.

THINK ABOUT IT

- Other than pride, what are some things that cause strong Christians to fall?

- Are your eyes on Jesus, or have you lost sight of what matters?

- How often do you pray for a strong finish?

PRAY ABOUT IT

- Ask God to guard you from the temptation to look away from Him when it matters the most.

- Pray for endurance and humility.

- Thank God for bringing you this far.

Lord, I'm nothing without Your strength.
Remind me of that whenever I start feeling boastful.

61.
COMEDY OF ERRORS

If we confess our sins, He is faithful and just to forgive us our sins and to cleanse us from all unrighteousness.
1 John 1:9 SKJV

If you've ever watched a humorous television show or movie, you know that much of the comedy often comes from watching the characters misunderstand each other to the point of absurdity. Just a little more open communication and the whole mess could be easily avoided, yet nobody on screen seems willing to sit down and talk it out.

How often do we treat our relationship with God the same way? In a plot twist that's so very *not* funny, many of us refuse to confess our errors, sticking to our guns even when it's obvious to us and everyone around that we've made the mistake of the century. Instead, we rationalize our decisions, going to great lengths to explain to ourselves why the sin we committed wasn't really a sin after all. So we continue on, pretending all is well, while the consequences of our stubbornness lead to a disaster.

Your life doesn't have to be a comedy of errors—the simple act of confession can clear away all your guilt. Peace is only a prayer away.

THINK ABOUT IT

- Why do you resist confession sometimes?

- Why do you think God requires repentance before salvation?

- How often do you examine yourself for blatant errors that might be hidden to you?

PRAY ABOUT IT

- Pray for the humility to bring mistakes before God.

- Admit any unconfessed sins.

- Ask God to help you value open communication with Him.

Thank You, Jesus, for making the process of forgiveness so easy. Help me to never overcomplicate things by refusing to confess.

62.
COMPROMISED

It is because of the LORD's mercies that we are not consumed, because His compassions do not fail.
LAMENTATIONS 3:22 SKJV

On June 18, 2023, a submersible vehicle operated by the tourism company OceanGate started its journey down to the wreckage of the *Titanic*, thirteen thousand feet under the sea. Despite numerous warnings about the safety of such an expedition, the submersible kept descending. . .until suddenly, in a single instant, a small compromise in the vehicle's hull caused the ship to implode violently. All five passengers died instantaneously beneath the crushing weight of the Atlantic Ocean.

Much like the ocean surrounding that doomed submersible, this world is an unforgiving place. To survive, we need to make sure our faith in God—the one whose mercy prevents our destruction—is intact at all times. The moment we stop praying and start letting sin seep into our lives is the moment our hull begins to strain. Unless we shore it up in humble faith, an implosion will follow.

Prayer is the only way to make sure your faith remains uncompromised. How sturdy is your hull?

THINK ABOUT IT

- Do you regularly check the integrity of your faith?
- What are some warning signs that a Christian's faith might be compromised?
- Are you willing to heed these warnings?

PRAY ABOUT IT

- Ask God to keep your spiritual hull strong whenever the pressure increases.
- Thank God for ensuring your safety.
- Pray that others will find the safety you've found before it's too late.

Lord, give me peace and protection in this dark, suffocating world. Help me maintain the integrity of my faith in You.

63.
ABSOLUTE ANARCHY

In those days there was no king in Israel,
but every man did what was right in his own eyes.
JUDGES 17:6 SKJV

The French Revolution was one of the most shocking periods in human history, culminating in what historians have dubbed "The Reign of Terror." After beheading the king, the citizens of France went on to execute seventeen thousand people. Anyone who was suspected of having connections to the aristocracy—at times, even children—faced the cold steel of the guillotine. The steady *clang* of its blade rang in the streets like clockwork for months, reminding everyone of the terror of absolute anarchy.

A life without God—a heart without the guiding power of prayer—would be strikingly similar. When we're not in constant communication with our all-wise, all-good Father, our base, violent instincts will attempt to lead us. Our relationships become tainted with hatred, and selfishness becomes our guiding principle.

Today, thank God for the peace and wisdom that prayer brings and make sure never to neglect the wonderful gift of faith.

THINK ABOUT IT

- Why might God remove His guidance when we fail to seek it?

- Are you actively praying for God's wisdom in your life?

- Why does the world's idea of "freedom" more closely resemble slavery?

PRAY ABOUT IT

- Ask God to be the King of your heart.

- In hard situations, pray for guidance and for the strength to follow it.

- Pray that God's wisdom will override your instincts whenever they clash.

Lord, I don't ever want to dethrone You in my heart. Without your guiding hand, my life would be nothing but chaos. Keep me grounded in Your love.

64.
BIG REQUEST

*"Give Your servant an understanding heart to judge
Your people, that I may discern between good and bad."*
1 KINGS 3:9 SKJV

If God came to you today with the words, "Ask me, and
I'll give you anything," what would you request? Would it
be for that new gaming console that just hit the shelves?
A new phone? A girlfriend? Or would it be something a
little less tangible, like influence among your friends or
recognition from the "cool" kids at your school?

Well, Solomon had that chance, and his reply was,
"Give me wisdom."

Wisdom? What difference would that make? The answer:
all the difference in the world. Without wisdom, Solomon
would have been overtaken by the greedy impulses that
accompany positions of power. He would have collapsed
into pride and spiritual rebellion, launching his kingdom into sin and chaos. But because Solomon prayed
for wisdom, God entrusted him with a vast supply of
resources—and the passion to use them for God's glory.

The Lord has promised you wisdom if you need it
(James 1:5). Will you make that request?

THINK ABOUT IT

- How much do you value wisdom?

- When it comes to your prayers, what's the ratio between prayers for guidance and prayers for physical things?

- How might you work on valuing what God wants you to value?

PRAY ABOUT IT

- Ask God to align your desires with His.

- Pray for an increased appreciation of spiritual gifts.

- Pray for the things you know from reading the Bible that God wants you to have.

Lord, out of all the things I can ask You for today, wisdom is the one thing I need the most. Teach me to crave Your truth.

65.
WHAT A DEAL!

*Buy truth, and do not sell it. Get wisdom
and teaching and understanding.*
PROVERBS 23:23 NLV

In 1991, Teri Horton was casually perusing the items at her local thrift shop when she came across an odd painting that consisted of random splotches and dribbles of color. Although she thought it was ugly, something about the painting piqued her curiosity. She laid down five dollars and took the piece home.

The work ended up being an absurdly expensive original by Jackson Pollock, the famous postmodern artist known for his chaotic canvases. Now, the estimated value of this piece is *fifty million* dollars.

We as Christians possess something even more valuable: God's gift of prayer. You have a hotline to heaven 24/7, the key to truth, wisdom, understanding, and any other spiritual gift a person could ask for. And it didn't even cost you five dollars—God gave you this gift freely. Be sure you use it.

THINK ABOUT IT

- What valuable insights have you gained through prayer?

- What steps can you take to ensure you never "sell" this gift?

- Why do you think God entrusted fallen humans with this invaluable opportunity?

PRAY ABOUT IT

- Ask God for the wisdom to know what to ask.

- Pray also for understanding.

- Pray that you'll never overlook God's answers.

Heavenly Father, I can't comprehend how valuable prayer is. . .yet You still encourage me to use it. Thank You for this amazing privilege.

66.
NO MATTER THE COST

There [Daniel] got down on his knees three
times each day, praying and giving thanks
to his God, as he had done before.
DANIEL 6:10 NLV

It was a dark time for anyone who still prayed to God.
The king, having signed a decree that nobody was to pray
to anyone but him, threatened all who disobeyed with
a gruesome death in a pit of hungry lions (verse 7). So
what did Daniel do in the face of this new development?

You guessed it: he *prayed*. Today's verse doesn't specify exactly what he prayed, other than the fact that he
gave thanks to God. What could Daniel possibly have been
thankful for? Was he really going to jump headlong into
the death penalty over a "thank You" prayer?

Yes! Daniel knew the importance of offering praise to
his Creator. It wasn't just a formality—it was a chance to
fulfill his life's purpose by praising the one who gave him
breath. And no king, no matter what sick threat he dreamed
up, could stop Daniel from doing so.

THINK ABOUT IT

- How important is gratitude to you?

- When God works in your life, how quick are you to thank Him?

- How can you train yourself to show thanks when gratitude seems impossible?

PRAY ABOUT IT

- Thank God for all the prayers He's answered.

- Thank Him for working behind the scenes to deliver you in the future.

- Pray for the desire to please God with your gratitude in every situation.

Gracious Lord, I'm not always as grateful as I should be, especially considering the ways You've blessed me. Help me value gratitude as much as Daniel did, no matter the cost.

67.
SAFE PLACE

*The Word of the Lord has stood the test. He is a
covering for all who go to Him for a safe place.*
PSALM 18:30 NLV

Everywhere you look, you can see evidence of spiritual disease and decay. A culture that once revered God's name now blasphemes it daily, and the very concept of hope has given way to a seeming acceptance of meaninglessness. Without God, this world has become a vacuum, draining the life and energy out of everyone it can, striving to make them as cold and dead as itself.

Prayer, however, is your lifeboat for navigating this empty void. If people at school are mocking God, ask for a reminder of His power, a revelation of Himself through His Word. When temptations blow around you like a hurricane, solidify your stance by praying for the willpower to endure.

God is a safe place in this dangerous world, and He invites you to take shelter in Him today. Prayer will take you there.

THINK ABOUT IT

- Do you ever feel worn down by the world's sinfulness?

- How often do you run to God for safety from spiritual corrosion?

- Why do you think God keeps us here, surrounded by sinful people and less-than-ideal conditions?

PRAY ABOUT IT

- Ask God to protect you from the world's influence, even when you can't see the danger.

- Pray for spiritual strength when you're tempted to compromise.

- Pray that God will return life to this spiritually dead culture.

Lord, I don't know how to navigate this world without losing my identity. That's why I'm determined to stay by You, the only one who can preserve my soul.

68.
PRAISE EVERY DAY

Thank God for His great Gift.
2 Corinthians 9:15 NLV

Thailand, June 23, 2018. A group of twelve young soccer players and one of their coaches decided to explore a cave after practice. When a sudden, heavy rain began to fall, their escape route was completely flooded. The group soon found itself trapped deep in the bowels of the earth.

Quickly, a massive rescue operation, consisting of thousands of people, began. They worked feverishly ahead of a coming monsoon, miraculously pulling the last of the team members out of the cave on July 10. But good news came with a cost: during the rescue process, on July 5, a Royal Thai Navy SEAL suffocated in the cave. Another died the following year from a blood infection obtained during the rescue. Lives were saved, but not without sacrifice.

When you pray today, thank Jesus for launching a miraculous mission to save you from the bowels of sin—a mission He knew would require His own death. Jesus pulled you out from certain doom and into eternal life. That's a powerful reason to offer praise every day.

THINK ABOUT IT

- Do you ever think of where you'd be without Jesus?

- How is Jesus' sacrifice even more effective than that of those Navy SEALs?

- What would have happened if Jesus had never come to earth?

PRAY ABOUT IT

- Thank Jesus for His unthinkable sacrifice.

- Pray that you'll never take this gift for granted.

- Pray for the passion to let others know about this amazing rescue.

Lord Jesus, I'll never be able to thank You enough for dying in my place. But even so, I'll praise You today and every day.

69.
UNASHAMED

*For I am not ashamed of the gospel of Christ, for it is the
power of God for salvation to everyone who believes.*
ROMANS 1:16 SKJV

It's no longer popular to be a practicing Christian. Of course, there are plenty of famous people who profess Jesus, and whether or not they're actually saved is between them and God. But if these people want to stay popular, they have to package the truth of salvation—that we're all sinners in need of rescue—in a vague, loosely defined message of "love." Why? Because anything else will come with a cost.

Today, be intentional in your relationship with Jesus, making sure to block out the world's opinions whenever they clash with His. When voices from your friends, celebrities, strangers on the internet, movies, songs, and even your own thoughts tell you to be ashamed of your identity, make time for a heartfelt conversation with your Savior. It's worth every effort to rediscover the immense value of your connection to Him.

THINK ABOUT IT

- When have you been tempted to hide your identity in Jesus? Why?

- Which is the more influential force in your life: culture or God's Word?

- In what ways can you be bolder in your relationship with Jesus?

PRAY ABOUT IT

- Each time the world drags you down, ask God to remind you of what really matters.

- Pray for the strength to stay on fire for truth in a world that's swamped with lies.

- Ask God to help you be more open about your faith, even if it costs you popularity.

Thank You, Jesus, for living in my heart as my Savior and friend. Help me to be as unashamed of You as You are of me.

70.
LIFELONG OFFERING

*Therefore I beseech you, brothers, by the mercies of God,
that you present your bodies as a living sacrifice, holy,
acceptable to God, which is your reasonable service.*
Romans 12:1 skjv

In Old Testament times, even the holiest of priests were separated from God's direct presence. Animal sacrifices formed the link between the people and God, so nobody was able to experience God's love firsthand. And as for a true relationship with Him? Well, the best title anyone could claim was "friend" (see: Abraham).

But with Jesus, all that changed. Now, God's direct intervention—the removal of guilt and the gaining of His approval—doesn't require sacrificial animals. No, *we* are the sacrifices now. Our lives—every word we speak and every action we take—serve as living, breathing offerings, reflections of the ultimate sacrifice Jesus made for us.

And as a result, we are not only free to enter His temple: we *are* His temple. Direct conversation with the Almighty is not only allowed but expected. This is no obligation but rather the greatest privilege of all!

Is your life a living sacrifice—a walking, talking offering to God? If not, how can you make it so?

THINK ABOUT IT

- Why is a Christian's sacrifice more than just giving up pleasurable things?

- How often do you think about your intimate connection with the Almighty?

- How does living as a sacrifice change a person's prayer life?

PRAY ABOUT IT

- Ask God to make your life an acceptable offering.

- Pray for the willingness to submit your desires to Him.

- Thank God for enabling such a direct connection with Him.

Father, I present my life as an offering to You, surrendering all my plans in exchange for Your matchless grace.

71.
THE RIGHT BALANCE

I say that we are not to put aside the loving-favor of God. If we could be made right with God by keeping the Law, then Christ died for nothing.
GALATIANS 2:21 NLV

Working for God to try to make up for the sins you've committed would be like snagging a fast-food position with the plans of paying off the national debt. It's a silly thought. There's no way you could ever pay those debts. You could never do enough.

But that shouldn't stop us as Christians from working for God. No, work will never save us. But our obedient service should flow from our love for Him, from gratitude for what He has done for us. There is a balance that we all need to find, and we reach that healthy place by praying for a Spirit-filled heart.

Today, ask God to give you the right attitude toward Christian service—not as a way to repay a debt but as a natural response to the payment He's already made.

THINK ABOUT IT

- Have you ever tried to work for your own salvation?

- Why are all such attempts futile?

- How do you think God feels about those who try to outdo Jesus' sacrifice?

PRAY ABOUT IT

- Thank God for doing for you what you could never do for yourself.

- Pray for the humility to accept this amazing gift.

- Ask Him to give you a passion to serve Him.

Lord, I want to serve You—not out of obligation but out of love. Fill me with this love and give me the ability to live for You.

72.
ANIMATING FORCE

Dear friends, you must become strong in your most holy faith. Let the Holy Spirit lead you as you pray.
JUDE 20 NLV

Today's verse implies that without the Holy Spirit's leading, even prayer will not be enough to maintain our walk with God. Why? Because we humans are a fallen, sinful bunch. Left to our own devices, we'll foolishly choose lifeless idols over a relationship with God every single time. Once that happens, prayer becomes something far worse than a formality—it becomes a mockery of the life we could have led had we allowed the Spirit to truly control us. Every prayer we pray becomes selfish in nature, and genuine praise is impossible.

But when you let God's Spirit into your life, prayer is the life-bringing fountain it was intended to be. When you close your eyes in conversation with God, your thoughts and attitudes will be guided by a power far beyond your own. God will give you the words to say, and He'll listen with sincere compassion as you pour out your heart.

Doesn't that sound like the best way to live?

THINK ABOUT IT

- In what ways can Christian teens open their lives to the influence of God's Spirit?

- Are you led by the Holy Spirit, or do your prayers stem from your own desires?

- What's the best way to tell which force is guiding your heart?

PRAY ABOUT IT

- Pray for God's Spirit to guide your conversations with Him.

- Don't settle for memorized requests— be spontaneous and honest in your prayers.

- Pray for your own inclinations to take a back seat to the Spirit's guidance.

Lord, I surrender every part of me, even the prayer I'm praying now. May Your Spirit be the animating force behind each plea.

73.
FAKE DEVOTION

"But no one knows the day or the hour."
MATTHEW 24:36 NLV

God knew exactly what He was doing when He refused to reveal the time of Jesus' Second Coming to us.

Imagine a world in which everyone knew exactly when it all would end. More than likely, most people would wait until approximately thirty minutes before the final trumpet to confess—and then only out of a last-ditch sense of duty and fear. Those who otherwise would have joined God's family purely out of a sense of appreciation for Jesus' sacrifice and a desire to be forgiven would probably put off their repentance until the end. There's just something about a lenient deadline that encourages procrastination.

But since obedience to God can never be on our own terms, this world would contain precious few souls who truly loved God. The final moments of this universe would be filled with fake devotion.

Thank God that we don't know when Jesus returns!

Today, pray as if each day might be your last, taking time to develop your connection to God before seeing Jesus face-to-face.

THINK ABOUT IT

- Why does uncertainty often strengthen our relationship with God?

- When are your prayers the strongest— when you feel you have everything under control or when the future looks murky?

- If Jesus came back right now, would He be a stranger to you? Why or why not?

PRAY ABOUT IT

- Ask Jesus to help you stay constantly alert for His coming.

- Pray for the endurance and wisdom to live each moment like it's your last.

- Pray that others will join God's family before it's too late.

Thank You, God, for giving me the chance to freely worship You. Help me to take advantage of these precious moments I have today.

74.
ALL THE WRONG PLACES

*Woe to those who go down to Egypt for help. . .but they
do not look to the Holy One of Israel or seek the LORD!*
ISAIAH 31:1 SKJV

You'd think that after hundreds of years of brutal slavery
in the land of Egypt, the Israelites would have appreciated
God's role in bringing them out. But alas, history often
repeats itself—even in the lives of people who should
know better.

Shortly after leading God's people across the Red Sea,
Moses was appalled to hear them yearning for their days
of bondage once again (Exodus 16:3). And in the centuries
that followed, God's people forgot their own history. They
displayed a terrible tendency to seek help anywhere but
in the one who'd brought them so far.

But don't we do the same thing? Each time we have
struggles—whether they're as minor as a test at school or
as major as a serious illness—we often turn to anything
but God for help. And then, when all options are exhausted,
we say, "Might as well," and grudgingly pray.

God doesn't want us to pray as a last resort. He should
be our first option. Only then will we find the success He
has planned for us.

THINK ABOUT IT

- When was the last time you turned to God for help *first*?

- What's the difference between seeking help from another person and putting your trust in that person?

- When our efforts succeed, who really deserves the praise?

PRAY ABOUT IT

- Pray that God will help you see His hand working behind the scenes.

- Ask Him for the faith to pray before you act.

- Pray that you never seek help in places God doesn't want you to go.

---

*Lord, You alone can help me. All others—
including myself—are just tools in Your
hand. Help me to rely wholly on You.*

75.
IT'S GOD'S WORLD

Be glad as you serve the Lord. Come before Him
with songs of joy. Know that the Lord is God.
It is He Who made us, and not we ourselves.
We are His people and the sheep of His field.
PSALM 100:2–3 NLV

For all of mankind's amazing achievements, it's sobering to consider all the things we still *haven't* done—and probably never will. For example, we've never sent a human being outside the solar system, explored the bottom of our own oceans, developed a cure for cancer, or found a way to create new life, even at a microscopic level. In short, this is God's world—we're just living in it.

Thankfully, our God is just as loving as He is powerful, and He wants nothing more than to hear His children call out His name in praise. We don't have to uncover the secrets of the universe in order to achieve purpose—our value lies in the image of God that lies within each one of us. . .and how we choose to respond to it.

Today, reach out to the Creator of all things. Praise Him for allowing you to partake in this vast, cosmic drama called life.

THINK ABOUT IT

- Why are even our most prized achievements not truly our own?

- How often do you contemplate God's infinite power and love?

- When was the last time you thanked Him for life itself?

PRAY ABOUT IT

- Ask God to increase your gratitude for things that most people take for granted.

- Pray for a proper understanding of His power in relation to yours.

- Thank God for allowing human beings to explore and understand portions of His creation.

Lord, my best achievement is nothing in the face of Your incomprehensible power. Thank You for this amazing world.

76.
RIGHTEOUSNESS— LOST AND FOUND

"How then can a man be right and good before God?. . . See, even the moon is not bright and the stars are not pure in His eyes."
JOB 25:4–5 NLV

The words in today's verses come from the mouth of Bildad—one of Job's friends who failed to console him, unsurprisingly, by giving remarkably bad advice. So it's wise to take what Bildad said with a grain of salt.

But in spite of the falsities found in his speeches, Bildad did have a point in this passage. On our own, it *is* impossible to be righteous before God—and his illustration about the moon and stars rings painfully true. What Bildad did not (and could not) see, however, was that God already had a plan in place to transfer His own righteousness to us—a legal transaction for the ages.

Through Jesus' sacrifice, our holiness is now only a prayer away. It doesn't matter how dirty you are or how badly you've sunk into the awful pits of sin—God is just as eager to answer your prayer for forgiveness as He is to answer the prayers His only Son offers for you today.

Through Jesus—and only through Him—can you be right and good before God.

THINK ABOUT IT

- How prone are you to feeling like you are beyond God's forgiveness?

- How does understanding the significance of Jesus' death alleviate those concerns?

- How often do you confess your sins?

PRAY ABOUT IT

- Thank God for doing the impossible and giving unrighteous humans the ability to find holiness.

- Pray that you'll never think of yourself as righteous without God.

- Pray for forgiveness each time you realize you've sinned.

Forgiving Father, I'm not worthy of Your grace, yet You give it to me anyway. Thank You.

77.
LOOSELY DEFINED LOVE

You yourselves are taught by God to love one another.
1 Thessalonians 4:9 skjv

Out of all the commands in the Bible, today's is by far the most important, the most often repeated, and the most difficult. But why is it so hard?

Well, for a number of reasons. Perhaps the biggest is that it's overwhelmingly easy to say, "I love everyone" and actually believe it. . .while treating everyone around you poorly. You may be concentrating so much on that one kind act you performed two years ago that you fail to notice your heart gradually growing cold, affecting your treatment of others in the present. Why? Because your definition of love is so vague that it's easy to apply the word to your life. *This command is for others*, you undoubtedly tell yourself. *Never for me.*

But in order to be properly shown, a Christian's idea of love should have clear goals. Each day should be an opportunity for self-reflection and prayer—a search for any sign of selfishness in the soul and a plea for God to reveal and eliminate it.

In order to love, you've first got to know what love is.

THINK ABOUT IT

- In what concrete ways do you display God's love to others?

- How can you improve your demonstration of true love?

- How often do you pray for God to reveal things about you that you don't realize about yourself?

PRAY ABOUT IT

- Ask God to give you a clear understanding of the form His love takes.

- Pray for the ability to feel this love. . .and to show it even when the feeling doesn't come.

- Thank God for showing this love to You.

Father, show me where I fail in loving others. Work inside my heart and increase my capacity for love.

78.
ONE BODY

And this I pray that your love may abound yet more and more in knowledge and in all judgment. . .that you may be sincere and without offense until the day of Christ.
PHILIPPIANS 1:9–10 SKJV

Have you ever sprained an ankle, broke a wrist, or injured some other part of your body? When that happens, other parts of your body jump in to help. Your uninjured foot does double duty; your good hand takes care of all the lifting. Without such teamwork, your whole life might screech to a halt.

Since all Christians are "the body of Christ" (1 Corinthians 12:27), we should all be very concerned about other members of the same body. That's what the apostle Paul taught in his letters. When one believer is down, the rest of us should lift up prayers as if we ourselves were hurting. When one is healed, we should rejoice in the knowledge that the body is well once again.

By praying for the well-being of others, you can fulfill a grand purpose. . .even when there's no way you can fill a physical, emotional, or financial need.

THINK ABOUT IT

- When you hear of someone hurting, do you feel that person's pain?

- Have you ever sensed the strain of other Christians struggling in their walk with God?

- How committed are you to being Christ's hands and feet?

PRAY ABOUT IT

- Associate with other Christian teens, listen to their struggles, and then bring them before God in prayer.

- Listen to the prayer requests given at church and incorporate them into your talks with God.

- Pray that you'll increase the effectiveness of Jesus' body on earth.

---

*Lord, I want to be a useful member of
Your body. Help me to strengthen
other members through prayer.*

79.
UNRULY MACHINE

Finally, brothers, whatever things are true,
whatever things are honest, whatever things
are just, whatever things are pure, whatever
things are lovely, whatever things are of
good report. . .think on these things.
PHILIPPIANS 4:8 SKJV

You're probably aware of stories in which a scientist builds an artificial intelligence, only to watch in horror as the machine goes on a rampage. In a simple act of oversight, the scientist allowed the machine's programming to escape its creator's control, resulting in absolute destruction.

Each one of us possesses something that's far more powerful than an AI program. . .and just as capable of slipping from our control. It's our minds.

If we fail to control our minds—if we neglect praying for God's guidance—our thoughts can soon lapse into destructive patterns. Anger, lust, envy, greed, and a host of other evils are all waiting to creep in without our awareness, hurting everyone around us—even ourselves. This makes self-reflective prayer all the more urgent.

On your own, you're not able to control your fallen nature. But with God's power inside you, it's absolutely possible to conquer this unruly machine.

THINK ABOUT IT

- How has your mental "programming" gotten the best of you?

- How often do you pray for better control over your thoughts?

- What's another way you can influence the state of your mind?

PRAY ABOUT IT

- Ask God to bring everything about you—even your thoughts—under His control.

- Pray for the ability to dwell on godliness, discarding thoughts that may lead to sin.

- Ask God to help you gain the mind of Christ.

Lord, I don't want my mind to become a swirling sea of godless emotions and impulses. Help me control my actions by first controlling my thoughts.

80.
SEAMLESSLY INTEGRATED

Now Boaz was seen coming from Bethlehem.
He said to the people gathering the grain,
"May the Lord be with you." And they said to
him, "May the Lord bring good to you."
RUTH 2:4 NLV

It's easy to read today's verse as a mere transition from one scene to the next, skimming over any truth that might be found within. But there is something important to be gleaned.

Notice how casual yet heartfelt the greetings are between Boaz and the ones gathering grain. To them, spirituality and everyday life were deeply connected and could not be separated. God's protection was deeply engrained in their hearts and lives, as evidenced by even the simple greetings they gave one another.

Wouldn't it be great if we could integrate prayer into our lives like this? If, whenever a problem arose, our first words were not a frustrated exclamation but rather a plea for God's help? If our thoughts toward others were always marked with prayer for their well-being and thanksgiving for their presence in our lives?

Such seamless integration isn't achievable overnight.

It can only come through years of dedication and—you guessed it—lots of prayer.

THINK ABOUT IT

- Does prayer come naturally to you? Why or why not?

- Are you intentional in your prayers, or do they just happen randomly?

- How might seamlessly integrated prayer change a person's life?

PRAY ABOUT IT

- Practice thanking God for everything—trivial and large.

- Pray for God to make conversation with Him a natural part of your life.

- Pray even when you don't feel like praying.

Father, I don't want my relationship with You to be built on scripted conversations or long periods without communication. Please help me to be intentional in my prayer life.

81.
ETERNAL CELEBRATION

"See! God's home is with men. He will live with them."
REVELATION 21:3 NLV

Some Christians go through life thinking, *As long as I make it to heaven, that's good enough for me.* But just think how absurd this attitude is. Imagine you've been invited to a banquet in the White House, and the president says you can invite your friends at school to tag along. You refuse, however, thinking, *I don't care who else goes—as long as I'm there, that's all that matters.*

How selfish! Not only are you depriving your friends of something you know they'd enjoy, but you're also ensuring that you won't encounter any familiar faces once you get there. Sure, the dinner might be fun. . .but just think of how much better it would be if you had people you could share it with.

Today, don't miss the chance to pray for the salvation of those who don't know God. Jesus died to make sure everyone has the opportunity to experience His love forever. Doesn't that sound like an experience worth sharing?

THINK ABOUT IT

- How many lost people do you know?

- Do you ever think of how tragic it would be if these people didn't make it to heaven?

- How can you heighten your urgency for people's salvation today?

PRAY ABOUT IT

- Ask God to reveal Himself to the people who don't know Him yet.

- Pray for the right words to say to those who may be considering God.

- Pray that your actions, words, and life will be an invitation for others to join you in heaven.

Lord, I can't thank You enough for inviting me to Your final banquet. Help me influence as many people as possible to join me in this eternal celebration.

82.
COSMIC CHECKMATE

"You have put all things in subjection under his feet."
. . . But now we do not yet see all things put under him.
HEBREWS 2:8 SKJV

To live in faith means accepting both the "already" and the "not yet."

What does that mean? It means knowing beyond a doubt that Jesus has *already* defeated evil once and for all. . .even when this victory has *not yet* arrived from our perspective. Like a chess master who already knows his opponent is trapped beyond all escape, Jesus has already initiated the cosmic checkmate. Now, it's just a matter of waiting for the pieces to fall as planned.

In our eyes, however, evil is alive and well. Satan seems to be winning battles left and right. But the closer we remain to God—the more often we commune with Him and experience His peace—the greater understanding we'll have about the final victory that awaits at the end of time.

Today, let prayer guide you into the *already*, giving you strength for the *not yet*.

THINK ABOUT IT

- Why do you think God hasn't revealed how and when the end will happen?

- How has God's plan unfolded in ways that have only become obvious to us centuries later?

- Do you think God's biggest victory (the payment for our sins) looked like a victory at the time? Why or why not?

PRAY ABOUT IT

- Ask God for patience in waiting for His plan to unfold.

- Pray that you'll never be too distracted by small defeats to notice the big victories.

- Pray for the chance to play your part in God's winning strategy.

Father, I'm not sure how my life will shake out. . .but I know where I'm going after it's over. Thank You for this overwhelming hope.

83.
JUST ASK!

The snake said to the woman, "No, you for sure will not die! For God knows that when you eat from [the forbidden tree], your eyes will be opened and you will be like God, knowing good and bad."
GENESIS 3:4–5 NLV

If Eve was fooled by the serpent's statement—if she truly believed at that moment that she had misunderstood God's request—what's the one thing she should've done? Well, God was right there walking in the first couple's midst (verse 8), so she should have *just asked*. "Hey, God! Is what this snake said really true?" She could have spared humanity countless generations of pain.

From the very beginning, God designed prayer as a way to clear up misunderstandings and receive His peace and truth. Concerned about what to do in a situation? Ask God to show you, then open His Word to hear His voice. Don't wait to pray until after you've messed up. Clear up the confusion preemptively. . .talk to God *now*.

THINK ABOUT IT

- Why do you think it's so hard for many Christians to remember to pray when they're in tight situations?

- Do you regularly ask God for direction?

- If so, do you listen to His answer even when it's something you might not want to hear?

PRAY ABOUT IT

- Thank God for not leaving us to struggle on our own.

- Pray for guidance at all times, even when you think you have everything under control.

- Pray that your ears will be open enough to hear His answer, no matter what form it takes.

All-knowing God, I don't want to make important decisions by the seat of my pants. Teach me to slow down, come to You, and listen for Your advice before I proceed.

84.
BORDERLESS LOVE

"You will have the same Law for the stranger and for the one born among you. For I am the Lord your God."
LEVITICUS 24:22 NLV

In a public setting, it's easy to treat some people with greater respect than others. If you see a friend at school struggling to open a door while carrying a load of books, it's no problem to walk over and help.

But what about when it's a total stranger? Or what if it's a guy who sits alone all the time, earning the title of *weirdo* from the people whose friendship you value? Do you cast aside what others might think and reach out to that person? Or do you just keep walking, hoping to gain the approval of your peer group?

Kindness should never be a limited resource—it should be an overflowing cup, pouring out onto everyone we meet. To reach that point of fullness, we've got to keep in touch with God, who has an unlimited supply.

Once you get to know Him, you'll find your double standards merging into one law: the law of borderless love.

THINK ABOUT IT

- How equally do you treat everyone you meet?
- What would the world be like if God loved some people more than others?
- To whom can you go out of your way to show kindness to today?

PRAY ABOUT IT

- Ask God to give you compassion toward everyone—even those you don't know.
- Pray that you'll only see the image of God in all people, not their social status.
- Pray for His boundary-erasing love.

Lord, thank You for loving me as much as You love the whole world. Give me the ability to show this kind of borderless love to others.

85.
CHASING CONTENTMENT

"I gave you Saul's family and Saul's wives into your care. I gave you the nations of Israel and Judah. And if this were too little, I would give you as much more. . . . You have killed Uriah the Hittite with the sword. You have taken his wife to be your wife."
2 Samuel 12:8–9 nlv

A financial study found something very interesting. The world's wealthiest people tended to think the people in their circles were richer. Only the poorest people generally escaped that "I'm falling behind" mindset.

This is easy to observe in real life. We see billionaires—those who you'd think should be content—making huge investments just to drive their net worth even further upward. And yet we also see poor, humble people—laborers, farmers, housewives—who show more contentment each day than the rich and famous could wish for in a lifetime.

Next time you feel yourself getting envious over someone's new phone or car, ask God to replace that desire for more with gratitude for what you have. As long as you have a thankful heart, whatever you have will always be enough.

THINK ABOUT IT

- Do you thank God for each good thing that happens to you?

- Why does having more never bring the satisfaction people hope for?

- How might David's story in 2 Samuel 12 have been different if he had thanked God for his blessings?

PRAY ABOUT IT

- Ask God for the contentment that lies solely in Him.

- Pray that God will never give you anything that will draw you away from Him.

- Pray for the ability to use what you have to bless others.

Lord, You gave Your life so I can have eternal life.
If that's not cause for contentment, nothing is.
Help me never to chase happiness in any other source.

86.
CONNECTING POWER

Christic is the head of the church which is His body.
COLOSSIANS 1:18 NLV

The human body is one of the most fascinating objects in the universe. Perhaps its most intriguing feature is the way our brains communicate with other parts of the body.

If you want to move your arm, your brain sends lightning-fast signals down through your muscles, and your arm sends signals to your brain in return. The speed of the air hitting your skin, the amount of energy left in your limbs, the weight of the object you're carrying, and thousands of other signals are all transmitted directly to the brain, which then adjusts the arm's movement accordingly with additional signals. If you were to sever the nerves connecting the arm to the brain, the limb would be worthless.

Well, today's verse says we are Jesus' body. . .and He is the brain (or "head"). Constant communication with Him is not only advised but necessary if we seek to accomplish anything. Cries for help, expressions of gratitude, pleas for guidance, and prayers of intercession—all are vital signals we can relay to Jesus each day. And in return, He will give us signals of His own by revealing the truths found in His Word.

THINK ABOUT IT

- How deeply are you connected to Jesus, like your brain is to your arm?

- How might you work on being more dependent on Jesus?

- How effective can a prayerless Christian be?

PRAY ABOUT IT

- Ask God to control every aspect of your life.

- Pray that each choice you make will find its origin in Him.

- Pray for a willingness to stay connected to Him, no matter the cost.

Thank You, Lord, for the connecting power of prayer.

87.
AWE AND WONDER

*For this Man was counted worthy of more glory
than Moses, since He who has built the house has
more honor than the house. For every house is built
by some man, but He who built all things is God.*
HEBREWS 3:3–4 SKJV

Have you ever been taken aback by the beauty of a land-scape? The power of a thunderstorm? The skill of a talented musician? The intelligence of a super-genius? Such feelings of awe in the face of things far beyond our normal experience are perfectly natural—a God-given reaction to expressions of His wisdom and might.

The problem comes, however, when we stop at those feelings—if we idolize the medium through which God's creativity flows rather than God Himself. In short, even innocent awe can become sinful when we praise the creation more than the Creator (Romans 1:25).

Our lips were created for songs of praise, and the passions in our hearts were made to provide the words. Feeling awe and refusing to praise, therefore, is a sign that the soul has forgotten its purpose.

THINK ABOUT IT

- What are some ways we can praise God for the beauty in this world?

- How can we keep our awe directed always at the Creator?

- What are some ways people misuse God's gift of awe and wonder?

PRAY ABOUT IT

- Every time you're amazed by something, thank God for placing it in your life.

- Pray for a better appreciation of the infinite skill that went into creating this world.

- Praise God for giving you the ability to feel awe.

Lord, may I never let my feelings of awe float aimlessly inside me—may they be like well-aimed arrows, always finding their mark in Your infinite creativity.

88.
LIKE DANIEL

" I have heard that the spirit of the gods is in you. Light and understanding and special wisdom have been found in you also."
DANIEL 5:14 NLV

King Belshazzar didn't quite know what it was, but he saw an understanding in young Daniel's heart that far eclipsed the supposed wisdom of his finest astrologers.

Reading the rest of the book of Daniel, it's easy to see that this wisdom came not from Daniel himself but from the God to whom he prayed each day—a topic we covered several pages back.

Daniel's prayers didn't go unanswered, and the reward for his devotion went beyond a mere pat on the back. God gave Daniel unheard-of levels of insight so that he might stand head and shoulders above the pagan priests of the day. But Daniel, being the godly man he was, never took credit for these revelations. Instead, he was careful to direct attention to the God from whom these insights flowed.

You're never too young to be like Daniel. You can be a light of prayer-fueled wisdom in a world that's in love with its own dark deceits.

THINK ABOUT IT

- If Daniel hadn't prayed each day, would God have blessed him with wisdom?

- How often do you pray to understand God's will?

- Why do otherwise intelligent people often lack godly wisdom?

PRAY ABOUT IT

- Ask God for the courage to be different.

- Pray that you'll know how to navigate the choppy waters of modern apathy toward the truth.

- Pray for God to use you to show His wisdom to others.

Lord, I don't have all the answers. . .and that's not what I'm asking for. I just need to know what You want me to know. Please grant me that necessary wisdom.

89.
SHOCKINGLY SIMPLE

"To make [the Levites] clean, put holy water on them that takes away sin. Let them cut all the hair from their body, and wash their clothes, and they shall be clean."
NUMBERS 8:7 NLV

When Christians embark on a plan to read through the Bible, the biggest hurdle is often the books of Leviticus and Numbers. Passages like today's—filled with archaic commands and cryptic rituals—dominate the narrative, and it's easy to just throw up our hands and say, "I'm not getting any of this." Then we jump over to Matthew.

But these passages are helpful precisely because of how archaic they seem. By peering into the old methods of cleansing and sanctification that God prescribed for His people back then, we can stand in amazement at how important Jesus' sacrifice is for us today. The difference is night and day—complex procedures and arbitrary rituals contrasted with the simple act of prayer.

Because of the work Jesus did on the cross, everything God calls us to—forgiveness, peace, holiness, and more—can be found by simply asking.

What an awesome system.

THINK ABOUT IT

- Put yourself in the shoes of the ancient Israelites as you read about what God expected from them. What would life have been like back then?

- Would you have been able to keep all these commands?

- Have you ever taken Jesus' new system for granted?

PRAY ABOUT IT

- Thank God for making the process of salvation so simple.

- Pray that you'll never try finding holiness in meaningless rituals.

- Pray for the ability to accept God's limitless grace each time you pray.

I'm amazed, God, at the difference between the Old and New Testaments. Teach me to appreciate this shockingly simple system of salvation.

90.
LIFEGUARD DUTY

*"The Son of Man has come to seek
and to save what was lost."*
LUKE 19:10 SKJV

There is a danger in knowing Jesus and enjoying His salvation. Sometimes we can view our flesh-and-blood neighbors as enemies—like they're the opposing side rather than candidates for recruitment.

Pride can make us think we are the standard of righteousness—while we do little to influence others to join us. We've been put on lifeguard duty, charged with rescuing as many people as possible. . .but sometimes we get too cozy in our elevated chair. We'd rather just blow the whistle at someone who's drowning than leap down and help.

Often, the best way to help someone—especially if that person is outside your range of influence—is to pray. Pray that God will use your life not as a standard to make others feel ashamed but as a lighthouse to guide people in the right direction. And most importantly, pray that God will show His light to them personally—just like He did to you.

THINK ABOUT IT

- Why is self-righteousness easier than compassion?

- Why is living a holy life solely for the praise of others problematic?

- How concerned are you with being an example?

PRAY ABOUT IT

- Pray for God to swap your complacency with urgency for the lost.

- Ask Him to help you understand the predicament these people are in.

- Pray that your witness will always be seasoned with love and grace.

Father, thank You for pulling me out of the water of sin. Motivate me to want to do the same for every lost soul I see.

91.
GOOD TEARS

"Blessed are those who mourn,
for they shall be comforted."
MATTHEW 5:4 SKJV

Near the end of Tolkien's *Return of the King*, Gandalf and Frodo are about to cross over the sea into the Grey Havens. As the ship prepares to depart, Gandalf says to Samwise Gamgee, Frodo's loyal friend, "I will not say, do not weep, for not all tears are an evil." And as the tears flow freely, Sam watches the ship slowly disappear from sight, pained by his loss but rejoicing in happiness that awaits Frodo beyond.

One of the biggest lies in today's churches is that God frowns upon us when we weep—that tears are a sign of faithlessness. Even Jesus wept (John 11:35), thus proving how natural genuine tears are.

When we weep, we shouldn't hide it from God; rather, we should talk openly about the thing that's squeezing the tears from our hearts. He will hear us, and He will store each sign of our grief in heaven forever (Psalm 56:8), making sure just one second of the joy we face at the end will outweigh the sum of our weeping here on earth.

And on that day, all tears will be dried forever (Revelation 21:4).

THINK ABOUT IT

- Do you try to hide your grief from God? Why or why not?

- In what ways is it healthy to openly display your grief?

- Why do you think God lets us experience grief in the first place?

PRAY ABOUT IT

- Thank God for making beauty from your tears, even when you can't see it yet.

- Pray that your sadness never teeters over the line into despair.

- Pray for God to give you hope in the middle of sadness.

Lord, thank You for making all grief temporary—and all promises of joy eternal.

92.
LOVE AT FIRST SIGHT

*"I have this against you, because you
have left your first love."*
REVELATION 2:4 SKJV

If you've ever been in a relationship, you know how exciting the first few weeks can be—it's like you've reached the pearly gates, and everything sad has suddenly been undone. It's a great feeling.

But human nature is such that even the most exciting relationships cool off. That's not necessarily a bad thing—nobody can live on an emotional high all the time. But we need to be careful that the normal moderating of our relationship doesn't go further and end up in apathy. It's up to us to decide whether we want the love to continue.

Today, examine your soul to see if the spark of love you originally felt toward Jesus is still there. If so, keep it burning through constant gratitude to God. But if not, pray these two things: (1) that God will rekindle the fire, and (2) that He'll reveal to you the reason you lost it along the way. . .so you'll never repeat that mistake again.

THINK ABOUT IT

- What are some reasons many Christians leave their "first love"?

- How can a Christian know when this happens?

- Why do you think God requires us to make some kind of effort to keep this love burning?

PRAY ABOUT IT

- Thank God for the amazing journey you began when you placed your trust in Jesus.

- Pray that your sense of wonder never flickers or dies.

- Pray that you'll always be attentive for any signs of wavering love.

Lord Jesus, Your love for me is eternal.
I want my love for You to be the same.
Strengthen my devotion with consistency.

93.
GREEDY PRAYERS

You ask and do not receive because you ask
wrongly, that you may spend it on your lusts.
JAMES 4:3 SKJV

At first glance, today's verse makes it sound like it's wrong to pray for your own needs. But as it turns out, there's a difference between praying for yourself and praying selfishly.

For example, think of the last time you were really sick. You probably prayed for God to make you well. . .and there's nothing wrong with that. Good health is a basic human need. But now imagine you have fifty dollars, and there's a new sixty-dollar video game that you're dying to play. You pray, "God, please cause someone to drop ten dollars on the street and help me find it before anyone else." Will God answer this prayer?

Probably not. In fact, the mere act of praying such a thing would show how improper your view of prayer is. Communication with God isn't like rubbing a magic lamp—it's a way to bolster your relationship with the Creator of the universe.

When you come before a holy God, selfishness and greed simply don't belong.

THINK ABOUT IT

- What's a good way of knowing if your prayers are selfish?

- Have you ever prayed to obtain something at the expense of someone else?

- How can praying selfishly become a form of blasphemy?

PRAY ABOUT IT

- Ask God to show you if your recent prayers have
- been selfish.

- Ask God to correct your view of prayer if necessary.

- Ask God to bless people you know.

Father, I never want to cheapen prayer by using it for unholy purposes. Teach me to pray only for things that are necessary for me or pleasing to You.

94

RESISTING NATURE

"Be holy to Me, for I the Lord am holy. I have divided you from the nations, so you belong to Me."
LEVITICUS 20:26 NLV

Being holy—being set apart for God—doesn't happen naturally. It takes the strength of God's will and yours, working together in harmony.

For an illustration, think of a rubber duck in a roaring river. It's tossed around violently, wherever the current takes it. Now imagine scooping up that duck and setting it on the slope of the riverbank. Now gravity takes over, and the little yellow guy tumbles back into the river. Why? Because a rubber duck has no power in itself—it is at the mercy of nature.

As a Christian—as a child of God indwelt with His Spirit and given the privilege of prayer—you have the power to resist nature. You can defend a classmate who's being bullied. You can say no to drugs and alcohol. You can stand up for your faith when others are mocking it.

God has scooped you out of the raging river of godless culture and set you in a safe, stable place. Today, pray for the ability to stay with Him. You never want to tumble back into the place He's already pulled you from.

THINK ABOUT IT

- Why do you think we're so naturally inclined to "fit in"?

- Is a Christian able to stay holy without prayer?

- Do you regularly pray for the willpower to be different from those around you?

PRAY ABOUT IT

- Ask God to help you see the long-term benefits of staying holy.

- Pray for the wisdom to see the end results of "going with the flow."

- Pray for the people who are still in the river.

---

*Lord, teach me how to walk with You
instead of simply flowing with the tide.*

95.
SAVED FROM DROWNING

He carried our sins in His own body
when He died on a cross.
1 PETER 2:24 NLV

In Missouri in 2019, a twenty-six-year-old Kansas man saw a woman struggling in the Elk River. He leaped into the water and managed to keep the young woman afloat. . .but the man himself drowned in the process.

Imagine if this woman, upon being rescued, chose to jump back into the river to her death. That would be strange and foolish, but also a slap in the face to the man who had just died saving her life.

Such is the way of those who return to sin after Jesus has saved them. Rather than living a life of gratitude and striving for the righteousness He made possible, they plunge back into death, crucifying Jesus in their hearts all over again (see Hebrews 6:6).

Today, thank Jesus for dying to save you from a death you deserved. He didn't have to do that, you know. Then pray that His selflessness will motivate you in everything you do.

THINK ABOUT IT

- Do you strive to avoid sin, or do you treat it too casually to care?

- How can gratitude help a person live a more holy life?

- How important is Jesus' death to you?

PRAY ABOUT IT

- Pray for God to reveal the weight of Jesus' sacrifice to you.

- Ask God for the desire to live the life made possible through Jesus' death.

- Thank Him for this second chance.

Lord, I don't know why You would die in my place. All I can do is thank You sincerely and surrender my life. May Your death for me never be in vain.

96.
INCORRUPTIBLE LEGACY

Asa did what was good and right in
the eyes of the Lord his God.
2 CHRONICLES 14:2 NLV

You're still young, so you probably don't give much thought to what you'll leave behind after you die. But the choices you're making now will, more than likely, carve out a path for the rest of your life.

At the end of everything, will it really matter if your obituary fills up the whole page? Will it really matter if your tombstone is thirty feet tall with striking engravings? Will it matter if people are impressed by the wealth you left behind?

Today's verse reveals the one thing that will actually matter after you die: the life you lived for God. This short scripture, which could be applied to even the most lowly person, is worth more than the records of all the kings and emperors in history.

Today, pray that your life journey is a path that leads others to God. Only then will your legacy be incorruptible.

THINK ABOUT IT

- Why is a good legacy hardly ever formed with a single action?

- Do you regularly consider the impression you're making on the world for God?

- How is prayer necessary for living an impactful life?

PRAY ABOUT IT

- Ask God to make you more conscientious about your legacy.

- Pray that each choice you make will serve as a guidepost for others down the line.

- Pray that God will use your life as an example of what it means to live for Him.

Father, I don't want my legacy to be about me. I want it to be a medium by which others come to know You. Help me to work on creating that legacy today.

97.
SOLVING FOR X

But there were false teachers among the people.
2 PETER 2:1 NLV

One basic law of logic says that two pieces of contradicting information can't be true at the same time. This rule is why your algebra class exists—without it, even the act of solving the equation $2 + x = 4$ would be impossible. What use would solving for x be if x could be anything?

Well, today's scripture describes a problem far bigger than the kind on an algebra test: false teachers and their lies. When we hear viewpoints that clash with God's Word, we know only one can be correct. And knowing that God cannot lie gives us the tools we need to find the solution.

When we pray for guidance, we're asking for God to open our eyes to the equation in front of us—to the missing piece that can only be filled with God's truth. And then, once we're willing to accept it, God will give us the answer. . .as well as the strength to plug it into our lives.

Beware of, but don't be afraid of, false teachers. Know that God has the solution, and the test is open book.

THINK ABOUT IT

- Why do you think so many people are deceived by "easy" questions regarding morality?

- How does the world's reasoning often only complicate the truth instead of clarifying it?

- How willing are you to accept God's solution?

PRAY ABOUT IT

- Pray for the wisdom to see the right course of action and the willingness to follow it.

- Thank God for making the truth accessible to us.

- Pray each time you feel morally conflicted.

Father, I want to pass Your test by studying Your textbook. Teach me how to solve problems using the laws You've given.

98.
GUILT AND APATHY

"My people are destroyed for lack of knowledge
because you have rejected knowledge."
Hosea 4:6 skjv

"My people are destroyed for lack of knowledge." Reading this for the first time, a person may stop and think, *Wow, God, not fair! Why are we judged for things we don't even know?*

If the verse ended there, this hypothetical skeptic may have a point. But it doesn't end there. The second half of the sentence says, "Because you have *rejected* knowledge" (emphasis added). There's a big difference between "I didn't know" and "I didn't care."

Prayer is one half of the God-given, two-step plan for obtaining knowledge. The other half being the study of His Word. Lots of people lack access to libraries or textbooks or scientific journals from which they can gain understanding. But everyone—from the youngest, poorest child to the richest adult on earth—has access to prayer.

By making wisdom and spiritual knowledge so easily obtainable, God has given us an enormous responsibility. . .as well as a breathtaking privilege.

How are you using this gift today?

THINK ABOUT IT

- In what other ways do people refuse knowledge?
- Have you ever failed to pray when making an important decision?
- How can you make sure you never refuse the knowledge God is offering you?

PRAY ABOUT IT

- Ask God to make you aware of opportunities to learn from Him.
- Pray for a keen spiritual eye that doesn't overlook God's wisdom.
- Pray for a desire to learn as much about God as possible.

All-knowing God, I know I'll never know as much as You. All I'm asking for is enough wisdom to help me get closer to Your will.

99.
BIG EXPECTATIONS. . .
BIGGER REALITY

A man named Lazarus was sick. He lived in the town of Bethany with his sisters, Mary and Martha. . . . The sisters sent word to Jesus, saying, "Lord, your friend is sick!"
JOHN 11:1, 3 NLV

When Mary and Martha sent for Jesus, they were probably expecting Him to arrive just in time, lay His hands on Lazarus, and heal him on the spot.

Instead, Lazarus died.

And when Jesus finally arrived four days later, Mary and Martha had already reached the second stage of grief. "Lord," Martha cried, "if You had been here, my brother would not have died" (verse 21 NLV). But what Jesus did next floored her and everyone present: He walked to Lazarus' tomb. . .and casually raised him from the dead.

If you ever find yourself praying through tears, wondering why God seems to be late to the party, keep in mind that His plan is far beyond your understanding. Your loss today will, the Bible assures you, result in your eternal gain if you only keep the faith (Romans 8:28).

THINK ABOUT IT

- If we're not sure what to pray for, does that mean we shouldn't pray?

- Were Mary and Martha wrong to pray for Lazarus' healing?

- How have your failures brought you closer to God?

PRAY ABOUT IT

- When sickness strikes you or a family member, pray fervently for healing, but always according to God's will.

- When tragedy strikes, thank God for eventually using it for good, even when you can't see how.

- Pray for God's will to be done, even if it directly contradicts your desires.

Lord, thank You for knowing and maintaining control of the future. I'm just along for the ride, eager to watch Your plan unfold.

100.
PRAY FOR PEACE

Grace and peace be to you from God our Father, and from the Lord Jesus Christ.
PHILIPPIANS 1:2 SKJV

You probably knew this already, but the world is on fire. War, disease, natural disasters, murder—pretty much every negative thing imaginable—are spreading rapidly around the globe. It's only a matter of time before they touch each of us.

But today's verse provides a remedy: pray for peace. Pray for peace within your own life, within the lives of your neighbors and friends, and within the lives of those Christians in third-world countries facing heavy persecution for their faith. Pray for the peace that comes not through an absence of suffering but through the calmness of pure devotion that's found in the center of pain. Pray for peace to outstrip the fires of destruction, strengthening souls and encouraging worn-down hearts.

Yes, the world is on fire and the devil is winning battles. But the Prince of Peace has already won the war. Today, pray for peace—and don't stop praying till it comes.

THINK ABOUT IT

- What's your reaction when you hear of terrible things on the news?

- How often do your prayers extend to those living across the globe?

- Why is peace impossible to find outside of Jesus?

PRAY ABOUT IT

- Ask God to grant peace to a friend you know is hurting right now.

- Pray for peace in the lives of those Christians who are mistreated for their faith.

- Pray for the peace to accept the past and look forward to the future.

Heavenly God, Your peace takes many forms, and I'm asking that You give us all a little bit of each today. This world so desperately needs it.

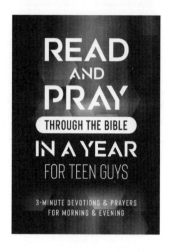